OUR LADY OF GUADALUPE
and her
MISSIONARY IMAGE

OUR LADY OF GUADALUPE
and her
MISSIONARY IMAGE

DANIEL J. LYNCH

The Missionary Image of Our Lady of Guadalupe, Inc.
26 Lake Street
St. Albans, Vermont 05478

Published by:

The Missionary Image of Our Lady of Guadalupe, Inc.
26 Lake Street
St. Albans, Vermont 05478
Second Edition 1996

All bible quotations are from the *New American Bible*, copyright 1970 and 1986.

Printed in the United States of America

Dedication

This book is dedicated to all those pro-lifers who have called upon Our Lady of Guadalupe as the Protectress of the Unborn to end abortion and convert millions as she ended human sacrifice and converted millions in sixteenth century Mexico.

It is dedicated to all of the Local Guardians of the Missionary Image who worked so diligently to make her Visitations to them fruitful.

It is dedicated to the staff of our apostolate who work tirelessly to enable Our Lady's Journey through the United States of America and the world by her Missionary Images. I thank the following for responding to her call: Joanne Batchelder, Robert McAuliffe, Christine Powers, Inge McNeill, George Ritchie, June Ritchie, Janice Flynn, Mariza Rubas, Peter Dulic, Gloria Dulic, Joyce Keen, Janice Keen, Sue Lynch, Kelly Lynch, Maggie Lynch, Lori Rainville, Sue Wimble and Carol Michaels.

It is dedicated to my wife Sue and family for patiently enduring my many absences from home.

Contents

Chapters

Contents

Foreword

This book is not a definitive scholarly work. It is intended to enkindle popular devotion to Our Lady of Guadalupe and to encourage a response to her recent call to end abortion and convert millions.

There are only a few Guadalupan publications in the English language. In fact, a major Guadalupan Bibliography listed 142 publications for the decade 1974-1984, and of them only 11 were in the English language!

Hopefully, this book will lead to a greater love and appreciation of Our Lady of Guadalupe, Queen and Mother of the Americas and, as the Immaculate Conception, Patroness of the United States of America.

Since a mother is not to be studied but to be loved, let us show our love for Our Lady of Guadalupe and respond to her request to honor her in the temple, the Church, and to recognize her as our Mother. She said that she is our "Merciful Mother, the Merciful Mother of all of you who live united in this land, and of all mankind, of all those who love me, of those who cry to me, of those who seek me, of those who have confidence in me."

The author submits to any final judgment that the Church makes regarding the recent messages of Our Lady of Guadalupe. In the meantime, we remember that Pope Urban VIII said, "In cases like this it is better to believe than not to believe, for if you believe, and it is proven true, you will be happy that you have believed, because our Holy Mother asked it. If you believe, and it should be proven false, you will receive all blessings as if it had been true, because you believed it to be true."

PART ONE

Pagan Aztec Mexico

1. Human Sacrifice

Imagine yourself as an Indian prisoner of the Aztecs in sixteenth century Mexico. You and your fellow prisoners have been slowly moving like cattle since dawn in one of four single-file lines, each of which stretches up to five miles long! The four lines lead to the four sides of a pyramid temple 130 feet high.

You hear the incessant beat of big snake-skinned drums. As you approach the temple base, you raise your eyes towards the top. You see 114 blood-stained steps and bloodied dead bodies cascading down them towards you. At the top you see witch doctors with never-cut long hair, matted in dried blood, clenching knives in their blood-stained hands.

You see them arch the backs of your fellow prisoners over four small stone altars, slice open their chests and rip out their still-beating hearts. One person is killed every fifteen seconds. The stench of death is unbearable.

You hear the jaguars in the zoos roaring in anticipation of eating whatever body parts are not eaten by the Aztecs themselves. You see the bloodied hearts burnt in human sacrifice in front of the Aztec idols. You await your fate without hope. Soon it will be your turn to be killed.

And soon it may be your turn to be killed today by euthanasia because of our complacency and toleration of human sacrifice by abortion. Your life is only as safe as the life of the unborn child. If the unborn child can be killed by abortion, then so can you be killed by euthanasia, which is the horrible logical consequence of abortion. If a mother can kill her child, then why can't a child kill her mother?

Satan had much power over the Aztecs in sixteenth century Mexico. They killed *80,000* people in human sacrifice in one four day orgy of killing in 1487 when they dedicated a new temple in Mexico City to their false god Huitzilopochtli.

This macabre human sacrifice was ended by the mercy of Jesus Christ who brought the Victory for Life through the intercession of Our Lady of Guadalupe. She will do the same for us today if we prayerfully seek her intercession in faith and confidence.

The Aztec society was much like our own. It was progressive in the knowledge of man but deficient in the knowledge of God. All of their human development was offset by their lack of development in the virtues. Mexico City, capital of the Aztec Empire, was the largest and most beautiful city in the entire world. The Aztecs had advanced far in mathematics, astronomy, architecture and engineering but they hadn't advanced in virtue. This was because they still practiced the horror of human sacrifice. So does our society by the practice of abortion.

The ancestors of the Aztecs had viewed a cataclysmic event in the sky. A great comet appeared in the shape of a fiery serpent. The comet later disappeared and the Indians believed that it had turned itself into the planet Venus, the Morning Star! They thought that it was a god and called it Quetzacoatl, meaning feathered serpent, because of its appearance as a flying serpent. They fashioned stone serpent idols after it and Huitzilopochtli, called the Lover of Hearts and Drinker of Blood. To these idols they offered human sacrifice.

The Aztecs had a pantheon of false gods and a complicated mythology. They worshiped celestial bodies and natural forces as gods. They offered them human victims in an idolatrous attempt to attract benign forces such as the sun, the moon, and rain; to bring health and victories and to avoid disasters. At least 50,000 victims were sacrificed to these grotesque idols each year. One out of every five children was sacrificed.

The ritual of human sacrifice was a satanic blasphemy of the Holy Sacrifice of the Mass. The Aztecs believed that their false gods (such as the Drinker of Blood) incessantly demanded the blood of victims which supposedly redeemed them from evil. But it was the blood of the True Victim Jesus Christ which truly redeemed all men from evil once and for all. His sacrifice is re-presented to us in the Mass.

In the year 1509, the darkness of pagan Aztec Mexico was pierced by the light of God. An Indian princess had a mystical experience. While she was in a coma, an angel with a black cross on his forehead led her to the ocean shore. There he showed her ships with white sails emblazoned with black crosses coming to the Aztec nation. The angel also told her that strangers would conquer the Aztec nation and bring them to the knowledge of the true God. She came out of her coma and related this strange experience to the Aztec rulers.

The princess' name was Papantzin, sister of the Aztec Emperor Montezuma. His tyrannical rule of the Aztec empire over the subjugated and oppressed Indian provinces of pre-Columbian Mexico was about to end. He brooded over his sister's prophecy and awaited his fate. The prophecy of Papantzin was soon to be realized.

A panoramic view of Tenochtitlan (Mexico City) as it existed prior to the Conquest of Cortes.
On the upper part is a representational mural. Below it is a model of the city. The pyramid in the center
was the High Temple at the top of which were the two temples dedicated to the false gods of Tlaloc,
the rain god, and Huitzilopochtli, the war god. The round temple was dedicated to Quetzacoatl.

The Sun Stone or Aztec Calendar. This once stood on a platform halfway up the High Temple. It is
3.57 meters in diameter and weighs 24.5 tons!
At the center is the grotesque face of the sun god, Tonatiuh, with his tongue lolling thirstily from his
mouth for the blood of human sacrifice. At the center of the base, the heads of two serpents meet. The
one on the left is Quetzacoatl.
With the destruction by the Spanish of the sculptures and images of the Aztec gods, the Sun Stone
was buried. In 1790, it was discovered. It is displayed now in the Mexican National Museum of Anthropology.

2. The Conquest of Cortes

Hernan Cortes was a Spanish soldier who had been running a small plantation in Cuba when the opportunity arose to lead an expedition to Mexico. In 1519, he came to the Aztec nation on ships with white sails emblazoned with black crosses just as Princess Papantzin had prophesied to Montezuma.

In that same year the Aztecs also expected the fulfillment of a prophecy that their god Quetzalcoatl would return to them in the flesh on April 22 to start a new era. This day was Good Friday in 1519 and it providentially happened to be the exact day that Cortes landed in Mexico. The coming of Cortes coincided with the fulfillment of Papantzin's prophecy and the prophecy of Quetzalcoatl's return in the flesh. The Aztecs thought that Cortes was Quetzalcoatl and that the Spaniards might be gods. Montezuma was unsure as to how to react to them and he was hesitant to engage them in combat.

This superstition aided Cortes' conquest of Mexico. He landed at age 33 with only 500 men, two priests and sixteen horses. He deliberately scuttled and sank his small fleet of eleven ships so that no one would desert him. This exhibited his great faith in the victory of Jesus Christ since he then had no means of retreat. With this motley army, led by Jesus Christ and the Sign of the Cross and sustained by his devotion to Our Lady, he defeated the Aztec nation.

5

Cortes marched upon the Aztec capital of Mexico City with his Indian allies who had lived in long subjugation to the Aztecs. Along the way his soldiers witnessed blood-stained temples and human sacrifice. One soldier counted 100,000 impaled human skulls on an enormous display rack!

Montezuma believed that he was confronted by an invincible godly force. In reality he was, but it was the invincible force of the One True God who led Cortes' army by the banner of the Cross emblazoned with Cortes' own words, "Brothers and Companions, let us follow the Sign of the Cross with true faith and in it we shall conquer."

In their first major battle, 300 Spanish soldiers defeated *30,000* Indian warriors! There is no explanation for this extraordinary victory other than divine intervention.

Later, Cortes was a guest in Mexico City during a truce. He saw the idol Huitzilopochtli at the top of the temple. This idol was fat with horrible eyes and snakes girded about its body and Indian faces and hearts around its neck. This was the idol before which 80,000 people were sacrificed in the four day orgy of 1487. Cortes demanded its removal. The witch doctors refused.

Cortes cried to God, "Why do you permit the Devil to be so grossly honored in this land?" He marched up the temple steps to the top platform and pierced the veil covering the idol. He then grabbed a metal bar and, according to an eyewitness, he supernaturally leapt up into the air and smote the idol's eyes saying, "We must risk something for God!"

He later cleansed the temple of its human blood, removed its idols and installed images of Our Lady, St. Christopher and the Cross. This marked the beginning of the end of human sacrifice in Aztec Mexico.

The Aztecs, led by their chief witch doctor, the Hummingbird Wizard, refused all peace offers from Cortes. They believed that their false gods would bring them victory. In 1521, they fought to the death in a ninety-three day siege of Mexico City which resulted in the wizard's dethronement, the annihilation of Mexico City and the conquest of Mexico.

Against overwhelming odds, Cortes and his Indian allies had conquered Mexico in the name of the Spanish King Charles who was soon thereafter elected as Holy Roman Emperor, the temporal guardian of all Christendom. Cortes said, "Our Lady was pleased to show His power and mercy, for with all our weakness we broke their arrogance and pride."

This conquest was an epochal achievement in realizing the claim of the Americas for God. This claim had been made by Christopher Columbus who had a divine mission to find the New World and convert the pagan natives. He had a special revelation concerning Isaiah's prophecy, "I will . . . send fugitives to the nations, . . . to the distant coastlands that have never heard of my fame, or seen my glory; and they shall proclaim my glory among the nations." Is 66:19. He fulfilled this prophecy and through his discoveries God's glory was proclaimed among the Americas even though much suffering was brought to the natives because of human sin.

Columbus returned from America to Spain and went to the shrine of Our Lady of Guadalupe in Estremadura barefoot and in sackcloth. There he gave thanks to Our Lady for his safe journey. This Shrine existed before the apparitions of Our Lady of Guadalupe in Mexico City.

Unfortunately, God's glory among the Americas and Cortes' hope for a new Spanish Christian civilization were not immediately realized. The Indians of Mexico were divided by languages and by the rugged terrain which made evangelization difficult. They thought Christianity was a "white man's religion." Moreover, their pagan beliefs were deeply rooted in their souls. Cortes had eliminated much of human sacrifice in practice but its belief was still held by many Indians and Baptisms were few.

Cortes wrote to King Charles and requested missionaries. In 1524, Franciscan priests came to Mexico and began to evangelize. These missionaries involved themselves in the lives of the Indians and preached to them the Good News that the

One True God was the Creator of all things and was a God of goodness and love who became man in Jesus Christ and died for them to free them from the power of Satan and to forgive their sins of the worship of false gods and the practice of human sacrifice.

However, the Spanish Establishment created a new social system that oppressed the Indians through slavery. This was due to their human greed and lust for power and glory. Slavery was justified by the argument that the Indians had no souls. The Spanish Establishment in Mexico did not follow the social justice teachings of the Church that the Indians were children of God with equal human dignity.

Bishop Zumarraga, first Bishop of the New World, was appointed Protector of the Indians by King Charles. However, the New Spain government in Mexico decreed that any Indian who appealed to him for help would be punished by death! After two of his priests were kidnapped and tortured by government agents, Bishop Zumarraga placed the entire city of Mexico under an interdict and excommunicated the leaders. Finally, in 1530 the King established a new government, issued a decree which prohibited slavery and confirmed Bishop Zumarraga as Protector of the Indians. An era of peace was about to begin, twelve years after the landing of Cortes.

But the Indians had no confidence in Spanish goodness. They saw the disunity of the Spaniards because of the difference between those who followed their religious teachings and those who practiced their irreligious politics. They saw this as the weakness of the Spaniards and were on the verge of a general insurrection. Bishop Zumarraga sensed this and prayed to Our Lady to intervene, to bring peace and a sign. He asked Our Lady to send him Castilian roses from his native homeland of Castile, Spain as a sign that his prayer had been heard. The stage was now set for Our Lady's entrance!

An artist's rendition showing Cortes installing a statue of Our Lady in the Aztec temple where he destroyed the Aztec idol.

3. The Apparitions of Our Lady of Guadalupe

On Saturday, December 9, 1531, which was then celebrated as the Feast of the Immaculate Conception, Juan Diego was walking on his nine mile journey to Mass near Mexico City. He was an Aztec Indian whose name in the Nahuatl language meant Singing Eagle. He had been baptized in the year 1525 at the age of 51 and was a widower who had a simple, childlike disposition.

At dawn, he neared Tepeyac Hill, the geographical midpoint of all of the Americas and the former site of a temple to Tonantzin, the false mother god of the Aztecs.

Suddenly, at the top of the hill he heard sweet bird-like singing and saw a white cloud surrounded by a magnificent rainbow. A brilliant white light shined from the cloud and he saw a beautiful young woman appear in front of it. She shined so gloriously as to make the nearby plants and rocks look like precious jewels.

The Lady affectionately addressed him, "Juanito, my son, where are you going?" He told her that he was on his way to Mass, and then she said: "Know for certain, dearest of my sons, that I am the perfect and perpetual Virgin Mary, Mother of the True God, through whom everything lives, the Lord of all things, who is Master of heaven and earth. I ardently desire that a temple be built here for me where I will show

9

and offer all my love, my compassion, my help and my protection to the people. I am your Merciful Mother, the Mother of all who live united in this land, and of all mankind, of all those who love me, of those who cry to me, of those who have confidence in me. Here I will hear their weeping and their sorrows, and will remedy and alleviate their sufferings, necessities and misfortunes. Therefore, in order to realize my intentions, go to the house of the Bishop of Mexico City and tell him that I sent you and that it is my desire to have a temple built here. Tell him all that you have seen and heard. Be assured that I shall be very grateful and will reward you for doing diligently what I have asked of you. Now that you have heard my words, my son, go and do everything as best as you can."

Our Lady had identified herself, stated her desire and gave Juan Diego his mission. This is the only apparition in which Our Lady identified herself by all five privileges conferred on her by God: her Immaculate Conception, her Perpetual Virginity, her Motherhood of God and of the Church and her Glorious Assumption.

Columbus had claimed the Americas for God and Cortes had conquered the power of Satan in His name. Our Lady now claimed the Americas and showed her love as the Merciful Mother of all of her children there and of all mankind. Our Lady's intervention was the connecting link which made the "white man's religion" the Indians' own. She wanted the former temple to Tonantzin at Tepeyac to be replaced by a temple to the One True God. She, the Mother of the True God, would replace Tonantzin, mother of the false gods.

Juan Diego went off to see Bishop Zumarraga to tell him this strange story. Understandably, the Bishop was hesitant to believe him and told him to come back another day. So Juan returned that evening to Tepeyac where Our Lady was waiting for him. He told her that he was not worthy to visit the Bishop and asked her to please send someone more worthy who the Bishop might believe. Our Lady kindly, but firmly, told him: "Listen to me, my dearest son, and understand that I have many servants and messengers whom I could charge with the delivery of my message. But it is altogether necessary that *you* should be the one to undertake this mission and that it be through *your* mediation and assistance that my wish should be accomplished. I urge you to go to the Bishop again tomorrow . . . . Tell him once again that it is the Ever-Virgin, Holy Mary, the Mother of God, who sends you to him."

So Juan trudged off to the Bishop again the next day. He patiently waited while the Bishop's functionaries kept him away from the Bishop. Juan's patience was rewarded and the Bishop heard his tale again. This time Bishop Zumarraga requested that Juan tell the Lady to provide a sign so that he could believe him before undertaking her request to erect a temple. Again Juan returned to Tepeyac where Our Lady assured him that she would provide the requested sign the next day. She said, "I will await you here. Do not forget me."

But Juan did forget her and instead of returning to Tepeyac the next day, he stayed home and cared for his dying uncle, Juan Bernardino. On the day after that, December 12th, he went off to get a priest to administer the Last Rites for his uncle.

As Juan approached Tepeyac Hill, he remembered that he forgot his appointment with Our Lady and he shamefully slinked on another way around the bottom of the hill in order to avoid her. But she came down from the hill and intercepted his path of travel. Again, she asked where he was going. "What path is this you are taking?" He tried to put her off with pleasantries. "My Lady, are you in good health?" Of course the glorified body of Our Lady was in good health! However, since Juan Bernardino was not, Juan Diego tried to excuse himself and told Our Lady that he was seeking a priest for him. She said: "Listen and let it penetrate your heart, my dear little son, do not be troubled or weighed down with grief. Do not fear any illness or vexation, anxiety or pain. Am I not here who am your Mother? Are you not under my shadow and protection? Am I not your fountain of life? Are you not in the folds of my mantle? In the crossing of my arms? Am I not of your own kind? Is there anything else that you need? Do not let the illness of your uncle worry you because he is not going to die of his sickness. At this very moment he is cured."

Our Lady had identified herself with Juan as his own kind, as his Mother and as the Mother of all humanity, the Mother of Life. She then told him to climb up the hill, pick the roses, gather them and bring them to her. This in itself required an act of faith by Juan since it was mid-winter on a barren hill where no flowers grew. However, he obeyed, climbed up the hill and found beautiful blooming Castilian roses which he picked, gathered and brought to Our Lady. Our Lady herself arranged them and placed them in his tilma, a long woven cactus fiber cloak, which was tied behind his neck.

miracle

Our Lady told Juan that the bouquet of roses was the sign that the Bishop had requested and that he should tell the Bishop all that had happened and all of her requests. She sent him off, in her words, as her "ambassador fully worthy of my confidence."

Once again, for the third and last time, Juan went off to see the Bishop. Again he was kept waiting a long time. Again his patience was rewarded. He entered the Bishop's presence, told him all that had happened and that Our Lady had given him the roses as the sign that he had requested. He opened his tilma with the words, "Here they are. Behold, receive them."

To Juan's astonishment, the Bishop fell to his knees in front of him as the roses cascaded to the ground. Juan followed the Bishop's eyes to his tilma and saw on it an image of Our Lady, just as she had appeared to him at Tepeyac! The Bishop with tear-stained cheeks then reverently took the tilma to his chapel before the Blessed Sacrament and begged forgiveness for his disbelief.

Our Lady had answered the Bishop's request for a sign with the roses which were native to Castile, Spain, the Bishop's homeland, augmented by the incomparable gift of her own portrait. Now it was the Bishop's turn to answer her request to build a temple.

The next day Juan Diego discovered that Our Lady had cured his uncle, just as she had said that she had, and identified herself to him as "Holy Mary of Guadalupe." Guadalupe was the name of a Marian shrine located in Spain. The Spanish name means "River of Light." Perhaps Our Lady meant to identify herself by this word as the River of Light of God, Mediatrix of all Graces, the Mother of the Spanish *and* of the Indians, in order to demonstrate their commonality as children of God equal in dignity. Or perhaps the word "Guadalupe" wasn't even used by Our Lady but rather a word in the Indian's Nahuatl language sounding like it and meaning "She Who Crushes the Serpent." This reminds us of the Aztec stone serpent idols which were crushed by Cortes and the serpent of Genesis who is Satan and who is crushed through Our Lady. See Gn 3:15; Rev 20:2. Then again, maybe God wants us to understand both meanings to Our Lady's title of "Guadalupe." Our Lady's choice of a name with almost identical Spanish and Nahuatl pronunciation with such significance to both peoples is something that only the Mother of all mankind could have done.

Bishop Zumarraga quickly responded to Our Lady's request and dedicated a simple shrine to her within two weeks. During the dedication celebration an Indian was accidentally shot and killed by an arrow through his neck. The faith-filled people brought the tilma to him and he was resurrected on the spot!

Word of these marvelous events spread like wildfire on the Indian grapevine. As Bishop Zumarraga wrote to Cortes, "In our day, God and His Blessed Mother deigned to shower the land which was won by you, with His great mercy."

Our Lady appears to Juan Diego on the top of Tepeyac Hill. Note his tilma tied around his neck, the singing birds, the barren hilltop and the cloud and round rainbow surrounding Our Lady.

Juan Diego tells the story of Our Lady's apparition to Bishop Zumarraga.

Juan Diego unfurls his tilma upon which Our Lady's portrait miraculously appears in front of Bishop Zumarraga.

Our Lady appears to the dying Juan Bernardino. She heals him and reveals her title as "Holy Mary of Guadalupe."

PART TWO

The Tilma

4. The Tilma As Our Lady's Portrait

Our Lady left her self-portrait impressed on Juan Diego's tilma. It is shown on the inside of the back cover in a photograph taken by film producer John Bird within five feet of the tilma. Our Lady's portrait was not painted. The tilma is coarse and not suitable to be painted upon. It has no painted undersizing or brush marks. There are no colors in the fibers of the tilma. It is the only work of art in the world not painted by human hands! Pope Pius XII said that the tilma was impressed by "brushes which were not of this earth." Our Lady's portrait was miraculously impressed onto the tilma. Kodak officials in Mexico declared in 1963 that the image appeared as a photographic overlay on the tilma!

The tilma was used by Juan as a cloak tied around the neck. It could be rolled up and tied to adjust to a person's height. The bottom could also be pulled up to the waist to form a large pouch to carry fruits and vegetables. The tilma was coarsely woven from maguey cactus, like burlap, and consisted of two strips each measuring approximately two feet by six feet which were lightly sewn together lengthwise down the middle. This seam may be seen running through the middle of the portrait. Our Lady's head is gently turned to the right to avoid this seam.

The tilma should have disintegrated and disappeared within thirty years of the apparition. Rather, it has been miraculously sustained day by day by Our Lady's intercession until today, over four hundred and sixty years later! For all of that time it has been displayed for public veneration at the apparition site in Mexico City.

Our Lady appears on the tilma as an olive-skinned young woman, four feet eight inches tall. She is clothed in Middle-Eastern dress of the time of Christ. However, the colors of the clothing are of an Aztec royal virgin. But she is pregnant, which is physically obvious and which is symbolized by the four-petaled flower (Nahui Ollin) over her womb and the sash which is wrapped around her body and tied above her womb. The Nahui Ollin symbolizes the center of the universe; the One True God and Christ Himself who was born through Our Lady. Recent gynecological measurements have determined that Our Lady's image on the tilma has the physical dimensions of a pregnant woman!

At her throat is a small golden brooch with a black cross in the center. This identifies her with the Catholic religion. Her figure is surrounded by golden rays and on her head is a faint crown. She stands in simple, humble prayer with the moon at her feet, stepping out with her flexed left knee, led by an angel.

She is the Apocalyptic pregnant Virgin Mother of God, clothed with the sun, with the moon at her feet and a crown on her head whose offspring Satan voraciously seeks. See Rev 12. But she crushes his head with her humble heel (see Gn 3:15) as symbolized by the darkened crescent moon which the Indians had worshiped as Quetzacoatl and upon which she stands.

Saint Michael the Archangel leads the battle (see Dn 12:1; Rev 12:7) and holds her mantle (symbol of heaven) and gown (symbol of earth) as she marches forward as Queen of heaven and earth. Her Immaculate Heart is filled with tender love for us and can be faintly seen in the discoloration within her left hand, with a small cross at its top, in the very center of her being.

There is a danger in reading too much symbolism into the tilma or in studying astronomical and astrological signs in it. These can distract us from our Mother. A mother is not to be studied too much but rather to be loved.

The portrait is very life-like. The facial expression is sublime, humble, tender, gentle and loving. The mere sight of it is enough to melt the hardest of hearts into affections of gratitude, of respect and of love. It has a beautiful grace of symmetry. The whole corresponds to the parts and the parts to the whole.

There is a controversy as to whether parts of the tilma's portrait have been added by human hands. A scientific infra-red radiation photographic investigation concluded that there were human additions. However, some of these additions were claimed to have been made *after* the painting of the replica which was used in the Battle of Lepanto in 1571. This replica contained *all* of the parts that we see on the tilma today. This replica still exists in Aveto, Italy.

It seems more likely then that *additions* were not made to the tilma but that *embellishments* were made by painting over some parts of it. These painted overlays may include the crown and the moon. But Our Lady's face has never been touched. Human embellishments should not outrage us or lead us to doubt. We should believe that God intended the tilma for us as it is embellished, a gift of divine and human hands.

The color of the mantle is a bright turquoise blue. The robe is colored pink. These colors are brilliant. Science cannot explain what produced them. If they had been painted, they would have faded long ago.

The image is opaque from the front but transparent from the back. The overall beauty of the tilma strikes the eye at a distance from which Our Lady seemingly appears through the colors. The portrait simply defies human explanation and is beyond human capabilities. No human painter can reproduce it. In short, it is a continuing miracle!

5. The Tilma and Science

The divine hand on the tilma is evident through studies of modern science. For example, when one person looks at another, the other's image is reflected mirror-like in the cornea of the person looking. The eyes of Our Lady in the tilma were photographically enlarged. They reveal the reflected images of several people. Scientists admit that it is humanly impossible to paint these tiny images.

Some of these images have been identified as Juan Diego, Bishop Zumarraga and his interpreter. These three people were all present when Our Lady's portrait appeared on the tilma! It was as if Our Lady herself was hiddenly present looking upon the scene and leaving the sign of her presence in the corneas of her eyes.

In 1956, five ophthalmologists examined Our Lady's eyes in the tilma and each said that they looked into a life-like human eye including the retina upon which each saw the image of a man whose hands were extended in front of him at waist level, palms upward, carrying something red. This may be Juan Diego with roses in his hands.

Recently, astronomers reproduced a map of the stars as they appeared in the sky on December 12, 1531, the date of the appearance of Our Lady's miraculous image. This star map was inverted and overlaid as a translucency over Our Lady's image. The stars on Our Lady's mantle exactly coincided with the stars on the star map from the point of view of someone looking down upon the stars from heaven!

Similarly, a translucency of Our Lady's image was superimposed on a topographical map of Central Mexico. The major mountain ranges on the map coincided with the golden filigree flowers on Our Lady's gown!

God reserved these phenomena for the twentieth century to demonstrate to scientific skeptics that the tilma is His miraculous gift. These are the crowning scientific validations of this miracle. In Our Lady's words, "Is there anything else that you need" in order to believe?

Scissor's handle encircles the face of Juan Diego which is reflected in Our Lady's right eye on the tilma.

Portrait of Juan Diego which shows a remarkable similarity to the reflection in Our Lady's right eye on the tilma.

6. The Tilma as Pictograph

The tilma spoke to the Indians as a pictograph or hieroglyphic. After Our Lady's apparitions, Juan Diego had retired with the tilma to his small hermitage next to the shrine "temple" that Bishop Zumarraga had erected at Our Lady's request. Here he lived for the rest of his life. And here the Indians came to venerate the tilma and listen to Juan repeat his story of Our Lady's apparitions and messages. He did this over and over again, thousands of times until his death at the age of seventy-four in 1548.

From looking at the tilma and listening to Juan, the Indians understood that they were not *adoring* Our Lady but *honoring* her as the pregnant Virgin Mother of the One True God. They saw that she came from the clouds of heaven escorted by an angel. They understood, however, that she was not God because her head was bowed in humility and her hands were joined in prayer interceding for them to the One True God. They heard that this God loved the world so much that He sent His only begotten Son, Jesus Christ, to die for them and that His death was sufficient for all mankind to be saved from hell so that human sacrifice was totally unnecessary and absolutely evil. Human sacrifice ended completely!

The Indians heard that Jesus died on the Cross, as shown on Our Lady's brooch, so that they might have eternal life.

See Jn 3:16. They saw that this was the same Cross that they had seen on the helmets of the Spanish Conquistadors and which they now embraced as their own.

They understood from the tilma that Our Lady, although not God, was very close to Him and was the vanquisher of the Aztec false gods of the sun, which she eclipsed and which radiated from behind her; the stars, which she wore on her mantle; and the moon, upon which she stood as conqueror of Quetzacoatl, the stone serpent idol. "Guadalupe" meant to the Indians in Nahautl, "She who crushes the serpent."

The stars signified the regenerating gifts of God and called the Indians to holy Baptism. Our Lady's hands joined in prayer separated her small finger from the other three which indicated that the Indians were called by her to believe in the One True God in Three Divine Persons.

Juan Diego told the Indians that Our Lady had come to Tepeyac as their Mother to replace the Aztec false mother god, Tonantzin, who formerly reigned there and to replace the Aztec religion with the one true faith. The Indians accepted Our Lady as their Mother and, like John the Apostle, took her into their hearts (see Jn 19:27) because she had told Juan, "I am of your own kind." The Indians sang that "the Virgin is one of us! Our Sovereign Lady is one of us!"

The news of Our Lady's apparitions, messages and wonders spread throughout the Indian world. The Indian's hearts were melted by the tender and consoling story. They renounced human sacrifice and their idols, their ferocity, superstition and polygamy. They were ready for conversion.

As the missionaries approached the Indian villages, whole families came out and begged to be baptized. As they had once lined up for natural death by human sacrifice, they now lined up for supernatural death to sin, by Baptism into the new life of Christ. A single missionary sometimes tirelessly baptized over a thousand Indians in a single day! Nine million Indians were converted to the one true faith within nine years of Our Lady's intervention on their behalf at Tepeyac Hill. This equates to approximately 3,000 conversions per day continuously for nine years. It was like a continual nine year Novena of Pentecosts since 3,000 were converted at the first Pentecost. See Acts 2:41.

This was a divine balancing act because millions of souls were lost to the true faith during this same period of time as a result of the Protestant so-called "Reformation" in Europe. It was as if Our Lady of Guadalupe had been transported from Europe to the desert in Mexico by an angel with the wings of an eagle, which appear beneath her image, in order to bring the faith to the Indians. See Rev 12:14.

Our Lady of Guadalupe appears on the tilma as a mestizo, a mixed breed of Indian and Spanish. This helped to unite these two races which intermarried forming "La Raza," the new race of the Mexican people.

Our Lady reconciled these former enemies and the new nation of Mexico was raised to equality with Europe in civilization, culture, religion, education and opportunity. A new Christian nation was personally formed through the gentle, loving intercession of Our Lady of Guadalupe!

"The Offering" is a statuary display at the base of Tepeyac Hill. It shows the Indian at the extreme left offering Aztec idols to Our Lady of Guadalupe.

Franciscans baptizing Indians during the conversions of millions.

7. The Tilma and Scripture

Our Lady of Guadalupe identified herself under her first and foremost title given to her by her Son who said, "Behold your Mother." Jn 19:27. She said "I am . . . the Mother of the True God . . . . I am your Merciful Mother, the Mother of all who live united in this land, and of all mankind . . . ." Our Lady is then the Mother of us all in the order of grace.

As the Second Vatican Council said in the *Dogmatic Constitution on the Church*, 62: "This motherhood of Mary in the order of grace continues uninterruptedly from the consent which she loyally gave at the Annunciation and which she sustained without wavering beneath the Cross, until the eternal fulfillment of all the elect. Taken up to heaven she did not lay aside this saving office but by her manifold intercession continues to bring us the gifts of eternal salvation. By her maternal charity, she cares for the brethren of her Son, who still journey on earth surrounded by dangers and difficulties, until they are led into their blessed home."

In his encyclical on Divine Mercy, Pope John Paul II describes this maternal charity of Mary: "This revelation is especially fruitful because in the Mother of God it is based upon the unique fact of her maternal heart, on the particular fitness to reach all those who most easily accept the merciful love of a mother. This is one of the great life-giving mysteries of

Christianity." *Rich in Mercy*, 9. Our Lady truly is our Merciful Mother just as she said she was to Juan Diego.

The second title which Jesus gave to Our Lady was "Woman." Jn 2:4. This title identifies her as the Woman of the Book of Genesis and the Woman of the Book of Revelation.

Our Lady's mission and power from the beginning has been as the "Woman" to crush the proud head of the serpent Satan. See Gn 3:15. God put enmity between him and the Woman and her offspring, who are those who bear witness to Jesus. See Gn 3:15; Rev 12:17. Our Lady is also the "Woman" hated by the dragon Satan who wages war against her offspring. See Rev 12:17.

Our Lady of Guadalupe is this "Woman" of Genesis and Revelation since she identified herself as "She who crushes the serpent," as is the Woman described in Genesis, and she appears in her image as the Woman described in Revelation. As described in the Book of Revelation (see Rev 12:1-2), she appears as a great sign in the sky, a woman clothed with the sun, with the moon under her feet, and on her head a crown of stars (which is now only faintly visible). She is pregnant with child.

This association of Our Lady of Guadalupe with chapter 12 of the Book of Revelation dates from 1648 when the historian Miguel Sanchez first wrote of it. The association was also made in poetry by the seventeenth century nun, Sister Juana Ines de la Cruz who wrote, "This marvel composed of flowers, Divine American Protectress who from a rose of Castile is transformed into a Mexican rose; she whose proud feet made the dragon humbly bend his neck at Patmos . . . ." Patmos was the Greek island where the Apostle John received the Book of Revelation.

Our Lady of Guadalupe is escorted in her image by St. Michael the Archangel who bears her on eagle's wings. St. Michael is associated in the Book of Revelation with the image of the Woman, Our Lady of Guadalupe. See Rev 12:7.

"The Woman was given the two wings of the great eagle . . . ." The great eagle is a symbol of the power and swiftness of divine help. See Ex 19:4; Dt 32:11; Is 40:31. This help is mediated to us by Our Lady of Guadalupe's intercession.

Our Lady of Guadalupe is also the Immaculate Conception. She appeared on the Feast Day of the Immaculate Conception and identified herself as "the *perfect* and perpetual Virgin Mary." When Juan Diego unfurled his tilma in front of Bishop Zumarraga, the Bishop exclaimed, "It is the Immaculate One!"

The Immaculate Conception is the Patroness of the United States of America as proclaimed by Pope Pius IX who granted the request of the American Bishops gathered for the Sixth Provincial Council of Baltimore in 1846. As such, the image of Our Lady of Guadalupe is the representation of our National Patroness, the Immaculate Conception.

The Immaculate Conception Church in Allentown, Pennsylvania was dedicated on October 5, 1974 as the National Shrine in honor of Our Lady of Guadalupe. On that occasion, Bishop Sidney Metzger said, "It is eminently fitting that Our Lady of Guadalupe is welcomed here because it is accepted as certain and evident that her painting represents the Immaculate Conception. This interpretation was authorized by Pope Benedict XIV who in a Papal Brief of 1754 does not hesitate to call Our Lady the Blessed Virgin Immaculate of Guadalupe."

8. The Tilma and Signs and Wonders

The greatest miracle of the tilma is its very existence today. It should have disintegrated and disappeared within thirty years of the apparition since it is made from natural cactus fiber. Rather, it has been miraculously sustained day by day through Our Lady's intercession until today over 460 years later!

For all of that time it has been displayed for public veneration at the apparition site in Mexico City. For the first 100 years the tilma hung unprotected in a small, damp, open-windowed chapel, exposed to the air and the smoke from thousands of votive candles. It was touched by millions of venerating hands, lips and even swords! Many plucked threads from the tilma as relics. In spite of this abuse, the tilma retained its integrity and the freshness of its colors.

The first miracle of God through the intercession of Our Lady of Guadalupe by means of her tilma was the resurrection of a dead Indian. The Indian had been accidentally killed by an arrow through his neck. The arrow had been shot by another jubilant Indian in the procession to enshrine the tilma in its first chapel at Tepeyac in December 1531. He was resurrected on the spot when the tilma was brought before him!

In 1545, a deadly plague that had killed 12,000 people in Mexico City immediately ceased when many children made a pilgrimage to Tepeyac to pray for deliverance before the tilma.

In 1565, Indians on the beach at Cebu in the Philippines dropped their weapons and made peace with a Spanish expedition under the leadership of Legaspi when a priest presented them with a replica of the tilma. As Our Lady had reconciled the Spanish and Aztec Indians in Mexico, so she also reconciled the Spanish and Filipino Indians and Christianity was established in the Philippines.

Similarly, Christianity was established among the Ladronas Islands in Oceania. Formerly these islands were known as the "Islands of the Thieves." After a replica of the tilma arrived, there were so many conversions that the islands became known as the Marianas, named after Mary.

In 1571, the Moslem naval fleet was defeated by the Christians in the Battle of Lepanto when the winds changed and drove the Moslem ships into one another as Admiral Andrea Doria prayed before a replica of the tilma on the Christian flagship. This decisive battle saved Western Christian civilization from domination by the Moslems. Pope Pius V declared October 7, the day of victory, as the feast day of Our Lady of the Rosary.

In 1634, a flood in Mexico City, which had drowned 30,000 people, ended after four years of prayer before the tilma. The tilma was conveyed by a procession of boats from Tepeyac to the Cathedral in Mexico City and remained there until the flood waters abated. Then it was returned to Tepeyac in a procession of thanksgiving.

In 1737, a plague of typhus, which had killed 700,000 people in Mexico, ended as Our Lady of Guadalupe was proclaimed Patroness of Mexico.

In 1791, the tilma was preserved from destruction when nitric acid, which was used to clean its gold frame, was accidentally spilled on it. The spill merely left what appears to be a watermark which is still visible in the upper right hand corner of the tilma.

On November 14, 1921, the tilma was miraculously preserved from destruction when a bomb exploded beneath it. Enemies of Our Lady had planted the bomb in a vase of flowers at the base of the tilma. The bomb exploded and cracked the marble altar and the stained glass windows throughout the Basilica. A bronze crucifix three feet long was bent over backwards but the tilma and its glass cover were unscathed.

In 1929, the miraculous image of Juan Diego was first detected in the eyes of the tilma.

In 1991, Frank Smocznski, President of the Queen of the Americas Guild, sent 60,000 holy cards of Our Lady of Guadalupe to the troops fighting Iraq in Operation Desert Storm. The Executive Assistant to the Chief of Chaplains of the Navy said, "I am sure that through her powerful intercession we were spared a long conflict with massive casualties."

So many miracles have occurred through veneration to Our Lady of Guadalupe that records are no longer kept by the Basilica Shrine.

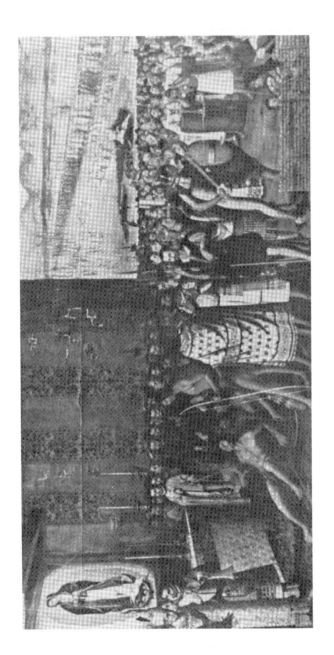

Painting of the "First Miracle" which shows in front of the tilma the resurrection of an Indian who had been killed by an arrow which had been accidently shot through his neck during the installation procession to Tepeyac Hill.
Note Bishop Zumarraga on the left wearing a miter, Juan Diego second from left to the right of the altar and Cortes in the middle holding a spear.

9. The Tilma and the Devotion of the Faithful

Devotion is the manifestation of our love, our honor and our respect for a person. The devotion to Our Lady of Guadalupe began from the moment Bishop Zumarraga fell to his knees when Juan Diego opened his tilma. The Bishop took the tilma to his private chapel where he venerated Our Lady's portrait before the Blessed Sacrament. From there it was moved to the Hermitage, the new temple that Our Lady had requested, which was erected at Tepeyac Hill within two weeks! The tilma was processed to the new chapel on December 26, 1531 by thousands of church and civil dignitaries, Indians and Spaniards.

Thousands of Indians and Spaniards soon came to the chapel to venerate Our Lady's portrait and to listen to Juan Diego relate the story of her apparitions and messages.

The tilma was venerated in the Hermitage from 1531 to 1622 when construction began on the Old Basilica. It was venerated in a temporary church until the completion of the Old Basilica in 1709. The New Basilica Shrine was dedicated on December 12, 1976, the Feast Day of Our Lady of Guadalupe.

These churches were built in response to Our Lady's expressed earnest wish "that a temple be built here to my honor. Here I will demonstrate, I will exhibit, I will give all my love, my compassion, my help and my protection to the people."

Our Lady requested a material church so that she, the Mother of the Church, could replace the false goddess Tontantzin and her temple and build us up as temples of the Holy Spirit in the spiritual Church, the mystical Body of Christ. Her love, help and protection for the people were demonstrated time after time.

Altars, shrines, statues and churches dedicated to Our Lady of Guadalupe spread from Mexico throughout the world to Italy, Spain, France, England, Sweden, Japan, Poland and the United States.

The United States National Shrine Center for Our Lady of Guadalupe, Patroness of the Americas, is the Immaculate Conception Church in Allentown, Pennsylvania.

There is a beautiful Chapel of Our Lady of Guadalupe in the National Shrine of the Immaculate Conception in Washington, D.C. On the walls are inscribed the words, "Who is she who comes forth like the rising dawn, fair as the moon, bright as the sun, like the rainbow gleaming amid luminous clouds, like the bloom of roses in the spring?" The altar depicts in mosaic the apparition of Our Lady of Guadalupe. The mosaic walls show streams of pilgrims coming to venerate her as they continue to do at the Basilica Shrine near Mexico City by the thousands daily and up to twenty million annually!

The Basilica Shrine holds 10,000 people and many more can see into it from the plaza outside. The Miraculous Image is enshrined behind bullet-proof glass with three frames of gold, silver and bronze. It is located on a wall behind the main altar twenty-five feet above three moving walkways which carry the pilgrims to view it from below.

More pilgrims go to the Basilica Shrine than any other religious place on the earth!

They come in throngs of a cross-section of humanity from all over the world, many finishing the last hundreds of yards of their pilgrimage on their knees. They have answered in confidence Our Lady's call to Juan Diego to bring her their love, their cries and their sorrows. She fulfills her promises and hears them. She remedies and alleviates their sufferings, necessities and misfortunes. All find something to love in Our Lady of Guadalupe who is the light that shines above the darkness of this age.

In 1992, America observed the 500th anniversary of the evangelization of the Americas begun by Columbus in 1492. The American Bishops entrusted this observance to Our Lady of Guadalupe and said in their pastoral letter *Heritage and Hope: Evangelization in America:* " . . . We entrust our observance of the quincentennial year, our commitment to giving birth with new fervor to the life of the Gospel in our hemisphere, to Our Lady of Guadalupe, Patroness of the Americas. She truly was the first Christ-bearer; by her maternal intercession, may her faithful sons and daughters be renewed and discover afresh the joy and splendor and promise of being bearers of the good news."

A panoramic view of the Old Basilica (right) and the New Basilica. Behind the Old Basilica is Tepeyac Hill.

Interior view of the New Basilica which shows the tilma in the center.

Fifth Centenary Cross, a replica of the Cross planted by Pope John Paul II at Santo Domingo, Dominican Republic. The replica is installed on the interior wall of the New Basilica. It is inscribed in Spanish, "Fifth Centenary of the Evangelization of the New World." The Fifth Centenary observance in the United States was entrusted by the Bishops to Our Lady of Guadalupe.

10. The Tilma and The Devotion of the Popes

In 1754, a priest related the story of the apparitions and messages of Our Lady of Guadalupe to Pope Benedict XIV in Rome. In a manner reminiscent of Juan Diego with Bishop Zumarraga, the priest completed his narration, unrolled a replica of the tilma and proclaimed to His Holiness, "Behold the Mother of God who deigned to be also the Mother of the Mexicans!" Like Bishop Zumarraga, the Pope knelt down in tears before the image and exclaimed, "For no other nation has He done this!" The Holy Father applied the words of the 147th Psalm to the nation of Mexico.

He immediately composed a Mass and Office for the Feast of Our Lady of Guadalupe, decreed December 12th as a Holy Day of Obligation in Mexico and commanded that Our Lady of Guadalupe be invoked as Principal Patroness and Protectress of Mexico. He also elevated the Basilica of Guadalupe to the rank of Lateran Basilica, co-equal with St. John Lateran in Rome as the church second in rank to St. Peter's of all Catholic churches in the entire world!

On October 12, 1895, the tilma was crowned as Queen of the Americas by order of Pope Leo XIII in the presence of forty bishops, hundreds of priests and thousands of the faithful.

On December 12, 1919, Pope Benedict XV proclaimed, "The Virgin of Guadalupe is the Protectress of the Pontiff."

In 1935, Pope Pius XI proclaimed Our Lady of Guadalupe as Patroness of the Philippine Islands.

On the 50th anniversary of Pope Leo XIII's crowning, October 12, 1945, Pope Pius XII ordered the image to be crowned again, proclaimed Our Lady of Guadalupe as "Empress of All the Americas" and said, "We are certain that as long as you are recognized as Queen and Mother, Mexico and the americas will be safe."

On October 12, 1961, at the close of a Marian Year of Our Lady of Guadalupe, Pope John XXIII prayed to her as "Mother of the Americas." This title was chosen because her apparitions occurred at the geographical mid-point of the Americas when the Americas were not divided into North, Central and South America and their various nations. She said that she was the Mother of "all of those who live united in this land."

Pope John also called her "Heavenly Missionary of the New World." Likewise, Pope John Paul II recognized her evangelistic role and in 1979, as the first pope to visit the Shrine of Our Lady of Guadalupe, he called her the "Star of Evangelization" and knelt before her image and invoked her assistance as "Mother of the Americas." His prayer to her on this occasion is contained in Appendix F.

Pope John Paul II stressed her evangelistic role again at St. Peter's Basilica in Rome on the 450th anniversary of the apparitions. On December 12, 1981, he talked about Our Lady leading us to Christ from the Basilica Shrine in Mexico City as a center "from which the light of the Gospel of Christ will shine out over the whole world by means of the miraculous image of His Mother." He prayed to her, "Since you are the Empress of the Americas, protect all the nations of the American continents and the ones that brought faith and love for you there."

On the same day, Cardinal Casaroli, the Papal Legate, was present at the Basilica Shrine representing the Pope. During his homily he said: "From that humble height the Virgin's eye turned to the immense expanses of the Americas, from the impassable peaks to the deep valleys, from the wind-swept plateaus to the boundless plains, as far as the extreme end of the continent, where the two oceans that surround it unite in a stormy embrace. It was as if the Mother's gentle smile illuminated them all with love and hope. Just as the sun, reflecting its brightness in the rivers and lakes, brings forth, as it were, new suns, so the Virgin's smile, beaming from Tepeyac Hill, seemed to be reflected in every part of this continent." He prayed to her: "O our Merciful Mother! From this house of yours and from all your sanctuaries scattered all over the Americas and throughout the world, lend your ears and your help to those who invoke you. O Mother of God and our Mother: give us peace! Amen."

Cardinal Casaroli also dedicated a statue of Pope John Paul II located on the Basilica grounds. He said: "Today we inaugurate this monument, which will perpetuate in your midst, in the Marian center of Mexico and of the Americas, his mild and beloved fatherly figure: Perhaps you do not need this, you who have carved his effigy in your hearts; but the monument is addressed to the future generations which will come here, so that they will remember that Pope John Paul II came here one day, a pilgrim like them, to lay his supplications and his hopes at the feet of Our Lady of Guadalupe."

One day when Pope John Paul II paused before a replica of the tilma he said, "I feel drawn to this picture of Our Lady of Guadalupe because her face is full of kindness and simplicity . . . it calls me."

He responded to this call and on May 6, 1990 he made another pilgrimage to the Basilica Shrine. There he proclaimed Juan Diego as "Blessed." On this occasion he said: "The Virgin chose him from among the most humble as the one to receive that loving and gracious manifestation of her which is the Guadalupe apparition. Her maternal face and her blessed image which she left us as a priceless gift is a permanent remembrance of this."

On May 12, 1992, Pope John Paul II dedicated a chapel to Our Lady of Guadalupe in St. Peter's Basilica in Rome below the main altar and near the tomb of St. Peter. He referred to Our Lady as the "star of evangelization and consequently the symbol of unity . . . ." He prayed, "Most Holy Virgin of Guadalupe, . . . always defend the gift of life, make truth and justice reign; promote industriousness and the Christian sharing of resources. May there be a joyous fulfillment of the civilization of love in the great family of the children of God. Amen."

Statue of Pope John Paul II erected on the grounds of the Basilica of Our Lady of Guadalupe. He is the only Pope who has visited the Basilica.

PART THREE

The Pagan Modern World

11. The Return of Quetzacoatl

Our Lady of Guadalupe has given recent messages to an elderly American gentleman as explained in Chapter 13. She said, "You and your home, the Americas, are being destroyed by pagan practices." See Appendix A, Sixth Message. The modern Americas have come full circle and have returned to worshipping Quetzacoatl, the Aztec false god.

Just as the Aztecs expected the return of Quetzacoatl in 1519, so too did his modern devotees expect his return on August 17, 1987. This was during the Marian year proclaimed by Pope John Paul II!

Quetzacoatl, the feathered serpent god, was worshipped by the Aztecs as the stone serpent. They also believed him to be a benign god incarnate in a man! His light supposedly swelled out from the center of the Americas and united all of its peoples. In the ninth century he purportedly prophesied periods of Thirteen Heavens and Nine Hells of 52 years each beginning in the year 843. The end of the Heavenly Periods and the beginning of the Hell Periods was supposed to occur on April 22, 1519, which was also Good Friday. This was the precise day that Cortes landed in Mexico. The prophecy continued that each succeeding Hell Period would be worse until the end of the Hell Periods on August 16, 1987.

At dawn on August 17, 1987, Quetzacoatl was supposed to rise again and return over the eastern ocean in the fullness of his power and might and bring his light, oneness and peace. At sunrise on that same morning, the heart of Quetzacoatl, which supposedly had been buried beneath an enormous ancient tree (the so-called Tree of Life) near Oaxaca, Mexico, was supposed to burst open sending billions of tiny spirits from the branches of the tree to implant themselves within the human hearts awaiting him.

It was for this reason that thousands of his devotees gathered and awaited him throughout the world on August 17, 1987 as part of the so-called Harmonic Convergence to usher in the New Age.

This transformation from the last Hell Period to the first Heavenly Period of the New Age was precisely preceded by the Feast of The Assumption of the Blessed Virgin Mary on August 15, 1987 during the Marian Year. She is the Woman Clothed with the Sun (see Rev 12:1) who is to crush the head of the serpent, Quetzacoatl (see Gn 3:15), and usher in the true New Age of the New Pentecost brought through the triumph of her Immaculate Heart. The New Age will not be brought by the heart of a false god who leads people into darkness, disunity and death although disguised as light, unity and life. Quetzacoatl is truly the Prince of Darkness and not the Lord of the Dawn, as his devotees call him.

The true light of Christ was brought to the Americas by Our Lady of Guadalupe, the River of Light, as the Morning Star preceding the true dawn of grace. She came to the center of the Americas as our Merciful Mother and truly united all of its peoples in the one true faith.

It is such pagan beliefs of the modern devotees of Quetzacoatl and others that have brought our age back to the darkness of pagan Aztec Mexico where our society now practices human sacrifice by abortion.

12.   Human Sacrifice by Abortion

The Aztec society practiced human sacrifice and the grossest abominations because they had no relationship to the One True God. Humans who live without a relationship to God will perform such abominable murders and even worse acts against the helpless innocents by abortion and infanticide.

This is where we find ourselves today, in a society that has no relationship to God and acts completely secular and humanistic. It is secular because it is worldly and it is humanistic because it acts solely by the power of man without cooperation with God. The name of its philosophy is Secular Humanism.

When the philosophy of Secular Humanism is applied to the law, it is called Legal Positivism which means that the law is whatever the judges say that it is, regardless of what God says.

The law of Secular Humanism can say that the sale of contraceptive devices is "legal," regardless if God says that contraception is an abomination. This is what the United States Supreme Court did in the case of *Griswold v. Connecticut* in 1958. This case which "legalized" contraception paved the way for "legalized" abortion in a parallel way that the actual practice of contraception paved the way for the practice of abortion.

The State of Connecticut had outlawed the sale of contraceptives, in accordance with God's law. But in the *Griswold* case the United States Supreme Court applied a "right of privacy" which they said is within the meaning of the United States Constitution, although it is not written there, and ruled that Connecticut could not ban the sale of contraceptives. The Supreme Court thereby "legalized" contraception and prepared the way for "legalized" abortion.

Similarly, the law of Secular Humanism can say that abortion is "legal", regardless if God says that it is an abomination. This is what the United States Supreme Court did in the case of *Roe v. Wade* in 1973.

The State of Texas and most other states had outlawed abortion in accordance with God's law. But in the *Roe* case the United States Supreme Court applied their "right of privacy" from the precedent of the *Griswold* case and ruled that no state can ban abortions. The Supreme Court "legalized" abortion and the millions of deaths of innocent unborn children that soon followed.

St. Thomas Aquinas said that any law contrary to God's law is no law at all. So slavery and abortion, although both were "legalized" by the United States Supreme Court, are contrary to God's law and, therefore, no law at all.

In the nineteenth century the United States Supreme Court failed to recognize slaves as persons within the protection of the United States Constitution in the *Dred Scott* decision. Now, in the twentieth century, the United States Supreme Court fails to recognize the unborn as persons within the protection of the United States Constitution. They exalt a "right of privacy" and "choice" over innocent human beings.

So that there is no doubt as to the humanity of the unborn from the moment of their conception, Jesus told an Italian mystic in 1943 about Mary's love for Him. Jesus said that: *"Immediately after conception,* O! What caresses she gave me, through her virginial flesh, while I was still shapeless and tiny, throbbing inside of her with my little embryonic heart! O! What heartbeats did I communicate to her heart through the obscure embryonic tissues, in the depths of that living tabernacle where I was taking shape in order to be born for you . . . ."

The United States Supreme Court's failure to recognize the life and personhood of the unborn reflects our society which worships the idol of "choice". It chooses personal human autonomy which is freedom from any restraints of God. But we should choose what is right and not what may be "legal", but what really is *wrong*. We should choose goodness, beauty and truth. However, our society has chosen evil, ugliness and the lie of "my body, my choice."

St. Paul, on the other hand, says that your bodies are *not* your own, but that they "have been purchased, at a price. So use your body for the glory of God." 1 Cor 6:20. Our bodies are really temples of the Holy Spirit (see 1 Cor 6:19) but our society has made them temples of Satan adoring him in their bodies through sexual sins and human sacrifice by abortion.

The year 1993 marked the 25th anniversary of Pope Paul VI's encyclical *Humanae Vitae* (On Human Life). In this encyclical he affirmed the beauty of married conjugal love as fully human, total, fruitful, faithful and exclusive until death.

He taught that there is an "inseparable connection, *willed by God* and unable to be broken by man on his own initiative, between the two meanings of the conjugal act: the unitive meaning and the procreative meaning." (No. 12). All such acts must unite only a validly married husband and a wife and must remain open to the transmission of new life. Therefore masturbation, intercourse before marriage or by those not validly married, artificial contraception, sterilization, and homosexual sexual acts are intrinsically evil.

As Pope Paul VI prophesied, the practice of artificial contraception led to marital infidelity, a lowering of morality and loss of respect by men for women so that many men consider women as a mere instrument of their selfish enjoyment. (No. 17).

In the end, the acceptance and practice of artificial contraception led to the acceptance and practice of abortion.

As the "legality" of artificial contraception led to the "legality" of abortion so too did the actual practice of artificial contraception lead to the practice of abortion as its natural consequence.

Our society, like the Aztec society, is progressive in the science of man but deficient in the science of God. All of our human development is offset by our lack of development in the virtues. This is because our society practices the horror of human sacrifice by abortion.

Our witch doctors are the abortionists. The only difference between them and the Aztec witch doctors is that the witch doctors killed more quickly but our abortionists kill more. The only principle that keeps a medical doctor from becoming a witch doctor is the Hippocratic Oath, named after the ethical ancient Greek physician Hippocrates. The Oath says, "I will not give to a woman an abortive remedy." Once a medical doctor *has* given an abortive remedy, he has crossed over the line and joined the witch doctors.

These modern witch doctors are even more evil than those of the Aztecs. They only killed thousands while ours kill millions! They killed to appease what they thought were idols greater than themselves while ours kill to satisfy only the idol of "choice."

The Aztec society "legalized" their human sacrifice just as our society has "legalized" human sacrifice by abortion. But what is legal is not necessarily what is right and abortion is clearly wrong. Just men ponder how to right such wrongs.

Cortes pondered how to right the wrong of human sacrifice and asked God, "Why do you permit the Devil to be so grossly honored in this land?" He said that "We must risk something for God!" Against insurmountable odds he conquered the society that "legalized" human sacrifice.

Modern revisionist historians say that he destroyed a beautiful Indian "civilization" and replaced the indigenous Indian culture with that of the "white man's culture."

In reality, this Indian "civilization" was like the whitewashed tombs castigated by Christ who said that they were "beautiful to look at on the outside but inside full of filth and dead men's bones." Mt 23:27.

This civilization was replaced by the Way, the Truth and the Life of Christ. A beautiful culture arose where the native Indians and the Spaniards cooperated in forming a new society of truth and justice which fulfilled all human needs and lasted 300 years. Unfortunately, a Secular Humanistic government replaced this culture in the last century. Mexico is now a poor third world country in spite of its great natural resources.

Other modern critics of Cortes ask whether he was involved in a just war. This is like the lawyer who asked Jesus, "And who is my neighbor?" Lk 10:29. Should those who know of the horrific evil of human sacrifice stand by and allow the killing of the innocent to continue because it is "legal?" Rather, isn't it unjust to do nothing? If we are able, shouldn't we do all in our power to prevent evil?

Cortes' actions were as just in 1519 as those of the Rescuers of the innocent unborn today who peacefully lay down their lives at abortion killing centers to prevent access of the abortionists to the mothers. Should we stand by and allow the killings to continue because it is "legal?" It is unjust to do nothing.

There was no alternative to stop the killing of the innocent victims of Aztec human sacrifice except by war. Cortes had exhausted all peace initiatives and the Aztecs had refused all of his offers. Today's Rescuers hope to eliminate human sacrifice the same as Cortes did. But they use peaceful means as an alternative to violence since, unlike Cortes, we are a part of the society that kills.

The Rescuers become as an unborn child, employ non-violent helpless means and place their bodies between the killer abortionists and the mothers in order to give each an opportunity to choose good and to avoid the evil of abortion.

The application of the criminal law of trespass against them is unjust since they justifiably trespass to prevent murder, a much greater evil than the simple inconvenience of the

Rescuer's bodies being located on private property. So, if they disobey man's law, it is good if they rather obey God's law. See Acts 4:19.

The Rescuers are like Shadrock, Mesach and Abednego who were sentenced to be burned alive because they "disobeyed the royal command and yielded their bodies rather than serve or worship any god except their own God." Dn 3:95. God's law says that "if you remain indifferent in time of adversity, your strength will depart from you. Rescue those who are being dragged to death, and from those tottering to execution withdraw not." Proverbs 24:10-11. To rescue the innocent unborn is an act of love and "there is no greater love than this: to lay down one's life for one's friends." Jn 15:13.

The efforts of the Rescuers have been prophetic. They have raised the consciousness of the people to the highest level ever in the Pro-Life Movement. They have forced everyone to take a position on the issue of abortion - either for or against, hot or cold. The lukewarm will be spewed out of the mouth of God. See Rev 3:15.

Nevertheless, the valiant efforts of the Rescuers and all of the other pro-life letter writers, lobbyists, picketers, marchers, counselors, etc. will not end abortion. None of these efforts have succeeded. Few legal gains have been made. Many gains that have been made in the legislature have been overturned and nullified by the courts. Like the human sacrifice of the Aztecs which Cortes almost eliminated in fact, but which remained in the hearts and souls of the idolizers, so too will abortion remain in the hearts of those who idolize "choice" even if abortion is once again outlawed.

As in 1531, we need a divine intervention today to melt the cold-hearted hearts of the idolizers of "choice." We need Our Lady of Guadalupe.

Abortion will end and conversions will come only through a moral miracle brought by the divine intervention of God through Our Lady's intercession and our use of God's supernatural weapons of prayer, sacrifice and the sacraments. A moral miracle exceeds human capabilities and is caused directly by God. We are His agents in causing this moral miracle in union with Our Lady of Guadalupe.

The way of her intervention has been prepared by the valiant sacrifices of all in the Pro-Life Movement, just as Cortes prepared the way for her intervention over 460 years ago. Our Lady told Fr. Gobbi of the Marian Movement of Priests: "On the Calvary of this century, Jesus is continually crucified and put to death in the millions of innocent babies, who are snatched from life while they are still in the wombs of their mothers . . . .

"On the Calvary of this century of yours, indifferent and cruel, Jesus repeats again his bloody passion. But beneath the Cross of this century, there is always your Sorrowful Mother. Like John, you too remain with me . . . .

"And let us keep watch in prayer, in hope, and in expectation . . . ."

Aztec human sacrifice by removal of still-beating heart.

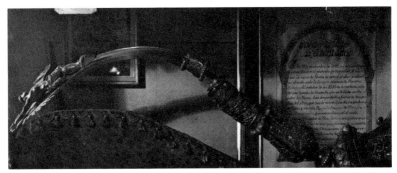

Crucifix from Old Basilica which is bent from a bomb blast over backwards like Aztec victim above.

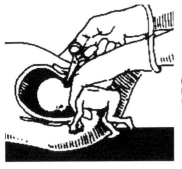

Modern bent victim of human sacrifice by DEX (dilation and extraction) abortion procedure which kills unborn babies up to 8 months old by stabbing them with scissors in their skulls.

PART FOUR

The Missionary Image of Our Lady of Guadalupe

13. Beginnings

On August 13, 1990, an elderly American gentleman heard an interior voice tell him, "Our Lady of Guadalupe wants to travel." In humility, he wishes to remain anonymous.

The next day, Our Lady of Guadalupe guided him to write a message from her. She wanted her Miraculous Image on Juan Diego's tilma to be released from the Basilica Shrine to journey in all states of the United States of America beginning at the International Rosary Congress at the National Cathedral of the Immaculate Conception in Washington, D.C. in June of 1991.

She wants the entire pro-life force placed under her banner as Our Lady of Guadalupe and she promises that together "we will end the horrible evil of abortion. I will help you stop all abortions. There will be no exceptions. Together we will bring about a new era of protecting all human life, that is, each person, from conception to natural death. I will put a stop to the present bloody human sacrifices like I did among the pagans after the miracle of my image began in 1531." She also promised to convert millions to her son, Jesus, just as she had done with the Aztec Indians. Later five more messages were given by Our Lady of Guadalupe. The messages are summarized as follows:

"I want to continue the mission I began in 1531. . . .

"As you go forth under my banner, as Your Lady of Guadalupe, you will have no better guide than what my faithful son, St. Louis de Montfort, recommends as the True Devotion to me. Through this devotion you will do all with me, in me, through me, and for me as I lead you, as always, to my Son Jesus and His Sacred Heart.

"Please pray for and support my beloved priests in the Marian Movement of Priests.

"I will send my angels to your side during all of your battles against the evil one and his works. . . .

"I want millions to see my image, the Woman clothed in the sun. I will melt their hearts to conversion. Through my Immaculate Heart I will lead them to the Sacred Heart of my Son. . . .

"You know of the millions of conversions following shortly after I gave my Image and how human sacrifice stopped. . . .

"It is the time for me to begin my Journey so all, in the Americas, may see me with their own eyes and know deeply the great love I have for each one of you, my children. You will have happen to you what happened to those millions of my children, one by one, so long ago." See Appendix A for the complete messages.

The first three messages of Our Lady were sent by the mystic to Father Walter Winrich, his spiritual director, who is an American Missionary priest in Mexico. He was moved by the messages and said that because they were received directly by the mystic with the faculty to understand and to feel, they were "more profound, more secure and less subject to error" than other kinds of interior and exterior locutions. This helped to comfort the mystic and confirmed that which he knew he had received from Our Lady.

In her Second Message, Our Lady said, "My first son on earth, my Pope, John Paul II, will help you in all the ways that only he can accomplish through his office as the successor of Peter. Go to him. Listen to him. He represents my Son Jesus on earth today."

On April 17, 1991, Pope John Paul II's assistant was personally handed the First Message by an American pilgrim in the Pope's presence. The next day the remaining messages from 1990 were given to the Pope's secretary.

Father Winrich translated the first three messages of Our Lady into Spanish and gave them to the Archbishop of the Yucatan, Manuel Castro Ruiz, who took them to Rome hoping to see the Holy Father. However, he was unable to see him because of time constraints brought on by the outbreak of war against Iraq in Operation Desert Storm.

So, Father Winrich then sent the messages to each Bishop of Mexico and, with his simple childlike heart, he invited each of them to come to the Basilica Shrine on February 24, 1991 to con-celebrate his 70th birthday Mass! None of them came but, like Juan Diego, he was undaunted and he tried again.

On March 11 he went to see a Mexican Bishop for a private audience. Like Juan Diego, he was kept waiting for three hours. Like Juan, he told the Bishop all that Our Lady of Guadalupe had said and her request for the release of the tilma. Like Juan, he was politely ignored and was about to be ushered out of the Bishop's office. However, unlike Juan, he "rudely" remained sitting. As the Bishop got up from his desk and was about to open the door for Father Winrich to leave, Father asked him, "Do you want the movement of the twenty-nine million Latins who have left the Church in the last ten years to continue?" The Bishop stopped dead in his tracks, returned to his desk, opened his notebook for addresses and suggested that Father see certain priests and to continue his mission to seek the release of the tilma.

On April 8, 1991, at the All-Mexican Bishops' Conference, Father Winrich met with Cardinal (then Archbishop) Juan Jesus Posadas Ocampo who suggested that he propose some plan other than the release of the original tilma.

An exact 4'x6' photographic replica of the original tilma was later given by the Catholics of Mexico through the Basilica

Shrine to go on the missionary journey. This replica had been placed twenty steps behind the original tilma in the Basilica Shrine and was made for the 450th anniversary of the apparitions on December 12, 1981.

All of this was done without any knowledge by the Mexican Bishops or Father Winrich that Our Lady had given a Fifth Message on April 17, 1991 for the Mexican Bishops which said: "Recently, I had requested that you release my image from that mid-point of the Americas so it could travel freely, being a means I have chosen to convert millions of my children to my Son Jesus. You know of the millions of conversions following shortly after I gave my image and how human sacrifice stopped. After thoughtful deliberation, you have judged that the release of my image cannot be permitted because of certain sensitivities involved. My sons, as the Magisterium in your land, your judgment will be obediently accepted by all who accept the authority my Son gave His Church. . . . My sons, Bishops of Mexico, there is a way you can meet my request. . . . Provide a replica of my image to the bishops of each country, territory and island of the Americas. As the replicas travel their paths out from my image, those paths become rays of my love, care, protection and help for all my children everywhere."

It is amazing that an exact photographic replica was provided without even knowing of Our Lady's request! The Miraculous Image was not released from its place of honor over the Basilica altar because it would have left millions of pilgrims extremely disappointed. Such removal would also have involved diplomatic considerations with the Mexican government. Therefore, the replica of the Miraculous Image was released which was called "The Missionary Image."

Our Lady of Guadalupe was sent in her Missionary Image as a ray of love from the Basilica Shrine as a gift from all Mexican Catholics to the United States through Monsignor Rogel and the Basilica Shrine because, in his words, "Our Lady wishes to use that image to help bring back to the Church of her Son the many millions of people who have left it. At the same time Our Lady wishes to end the horrible crime of abortions." See Appendix B for the Mexican Bishops' and Basilica's Prayers.

Cardinal Posadas blessed "from the heart this evangelical project proposed for the countries of our American continent, with the happy idea of carrying the image of Our Lady of Guadalupe, Star of the mission that was initiated under her protection five hundred years ago.

"I congratulate all the promoters of such a praiseworthy initiative and with pleasure I commend them to the hands of Our Lord."

He personally composed a prayer on petition and on behalf of all of the Mexican Bishops and prayed: "Mother of the True God, and Our Mother, Lady of Guadalupe, we beg you that your trip through all the Americas be realized now beginning with the Marian Congress of the Rosary in the National Sanctuary of the Immaculate Conception in Washington, D.C., the next month of June. We know that you want to end abortion in the world and convert twenty-nine million Latins who have left the Church and have taken themselves over to the sects. Lady, help us support your mission with our prayers in order that your Missionary Image will be well received in all the Americas."

Cardinal Posadas had recognized Our Lady of Guadalupe's evangelistic role as Pope John Paul II had prophesied when he said that the Guadalupe Shrine would be a center "from which the light of the Gospel of Christ will shine out over the whole world by means of the Miraculous Image of His Mother." The Cardinal called her image a "Missionary Image."

At Fatima on May 13, 1991, the tenth anniversary of Our Lady's protection from his assassination attempt, Pope John Paul II recognized Our Lady's mission. He too called her a "*missionary* on the earth's roads towards the awaited third Christian millenium. . . ." He prayed that she would "help us to defend life, a reflection of divine life, help us to defend it always . . . ."

Pope John Paul II is about to greet pilgrim Robert Bentley who holds the first of Our Lady of Guadalupe's recent messages which was presented to the Pope's assistant.

Monsignor Schulenburg, Abbot of the Basilica of Our Lady of Guadalupe, blessing the Missionary Image and author.

Cardinal Posadas of Guadalajara, Mexico with Fr. Walter Winrich reviewing the Cardinal's prayer for the Missionary Image.

14. Guardian Witness

The question that I'm most often asked is, "How did you come to be the Guardian of the Missionary Image of Our Lady of Guadalupe?"

Our Lady of Guadalupe said in her recent messages that together with us she would end the horrible evil of abortion without exceptions and melt the hearts of millions to conversion. She wanted all pro-life forces to join together under her banner and she said as we went forth under this banner we would have no better guide than St. Louis de Montfort's *True Devotion*. She asked us to please pray for her priests of the Marian Movement of Priests. See Appendix A for the complete messages.

These messages were sent to me by a friend and I was very encouraged when I received them because I was very involved with the interests that they addressed. I was involved with the Pro-Life Movement, with Our Lady of Guadalupe, with St. Louis de Montfort and with the Marian Movement of Priests. These four interests were the connecting links for my involvement with the Missionary Image. Because of them and my belief that Our Lady was calling me, I contacted the mystic who received the messages. I met him and Father Walter Winrich, his spiritual director, in June of 1991 at the International Rosary Congress in Washington, D.C. This was when the Missionary

Image first arrived from the Basilica Shrine in Mexico. Other apostolates volunteered to co-ordinate her journey and I also volunteered. The mystic, Father Winrich and myself had the same general vision for the new apostolate and they chose me to be the Guardian.

The first connecting link for my involvement with the Missionary Image was Our Lady of Guadalupe. In 1978, I first learned of her when I became involved in the Pro-Life Movement and discovered that she was pregnant in her image. I saw that as a very powerful pro-life symbol. Then I read Chapter 12 of the Book of Revelation regarding the Great Sign which appeared in the sky, the Woman Clothed with the Sun who was pregnant with child with the moon at her feet. It was in this image that Our Lady of Guadalupe appeared. I began to see the connection there and recalled that she revealed to Father Gobbi of the Marian Movement of Priests that she is the Woman Clothed with the Sun. She told him to read Chapter 12 of the Book of Revelation because we are living the times that are prophesied there.

I then acquired an image of Our Lady of Guadalupe and placed it on a wall above my desk. Every day I would pass by her and say, "Stop abortions and bring us a Juan Diego for today," in order to end abortion and convert millions. I prayed this prayer for years. In her recent messages she promised to end abortion and convert millions. This will be an answer to my prayer.

In 1987, I decided to join a Rescue and block an abortion killing center's doors in order to prevent a doctor from having access to the mothers, to be a last barrier for the lives of unborn babies, to plead with the mothers to save their children and to pray to Our Lady for their conversion. I made a fool of myself for Christ. I wore a big red beret to symbolize all the innocent blood that had been spilled. I wore a full-sized Brown Scapular and in its middle I placed an Image of Our Lady of Guadalupe. I was arrested and thrown into a Vermont jail at the feet of Joan Andrews Bell. She had spent 2½ years in solitary confinement in Florida for rescuing unborn children.

I was in a lot of pain from the handcuffs which the police had deliberately overly tightened. Because of this, I had my eyes closed and I laid there in prayer as Our Lady of Guadalupe was exposed on my chest.

Then I heard this sweet voice singing "Hail Mary." Joan started it and the whole jail joined the singing and I looked up and saw Joan staring at Our Lady of Guadalupe on my chest and singing Our Lady's song. That is how I began with Our Lady of Guadalupe in the Pro-Life Movement. I always prayed to her as the Protectress of the Unborn. The other connecting links with my involvement with the Missionary Image soon followed.

In 1988, I wrote a book entitled *The Call to Total Consecration to the Immaculate Heart of Mary*. This book explains the True Devotion by St. Louis de Montfort and the call for consecration from Fatima, Medjugorje and the Marian Movement of Priests. I was also the American lawyer for the Marian Movement of Priests and prayed for them as Our Lady of Guadalupe requested in her recent messages.

Finally, in 1990 I designed a banner with a prayer emblazoned around her image: "Our Lady of Guadalupe, Protectress of the Unborn, Pray for Us." This banner led pro-life forces in processions to abortion killing centers in lawful, peaceful, prayerful reparation.

When I later read that Our Lady of Guadalupe requested that all pro-life forces join under her banner with St. Louis' True Devotion as our guide and to pray for the priests of the Marian Movement of Priests, I discerned that her messages were calling me because I had already responded to these requests. It seemed only natural to respond to her call and to volunteer to be the Guardian of her Missionary Image.

15. The Journey Visitations

General Visitations. On June 14, 1991, the Missionary Image began its Journey of Visitations throughout the world. The Image arrived at the International Rosary Congress at the National Shrine of the Immaculate Conception in Washington, D.C. From there it has travelled throughout the United States and the world on Visitations under my direction as National Guardian.

I also entrust a Missionary Image to Local Guardian Teams who are formed to welcome a Visitation of the Image. They prayerfully prepare for Our Lady's Visitation through the intercession of St. Joseph who is the patron saint of our apostolate. Our Lady herself chooses and forms the Guardian Teams into families. The months of planning and prayerful preparation brings them closer together so that their hearts intertwine as they develop a deeper love for their heavenly Mother and each other as her children.

One Guardian was truly amazed at how Our Lady let her know what she wanted her to do during her Visitation. "She even awoke me in the middle of the night on her way here," she reported. "I was feeling badly thinking about her on a plane packed in a case and I felt her say to my heart 'not to worry, I visited my cousin Elizabeth on the back of a donkey, so the airplane will do just fine.' As the Federal Express truck drove up to my front door with the Image, hundreds of birds began singing (although I didn't see any around) and the church bells began to ring (although it was only 11:20 a.m.) and a priest drove up all at the same time! It was just glorious."

All of the Visitation liturgical events are coordinated with the local pastors and the Bishops. The Guardian Teams often receive Our Lady in awe as did her cousin Elizabeth and in spirit they cry out with her, "How is it that I should be honored with a visit from the Mother of my Lord?" Lk 1:43.

The Visitations often include churches, abortion killing centers, monastaries, convents, prisons, hospitals, nursing homes and schools. Hundreds of thousands have venerated the Image on its non-stop Journey.

All of Our Lady's Visitations in her Missionary Image are well received. The liturgies are reverential and well attended with inspired preaching. There are Masses, Benedictions, Novenas, Rosaries, and public veneration of the Image. The faithful gently touch and kiss the Image and place their religious articles on it and their petitions in a petition basket. Often there is all-night veneration of the Image with exposition and adoration of the Blessed Sacrament. Our Lady has moved the hearts of many priests to expose Our Lord where He has not been exposed in many years. There have been beautiful children's liturgies, many including the children's dramatization of the apparitions of Our Lady of Guadalupe to Juan Diego.

In her Image, Our Lady has visited prisons where hardened convicts have broken down before her in veneration. She said that she would "melt hearts" and she does. She has been taken to many nursing homes and hospitals visiting the sick in their rooms. Miraculous healings have occurred.

The Image has been brought to hundreds of abortion killing centers in a lawful, peaceful, prayer presence where the Exorcism Prayer of Pope Leo XIII's "Prayer against Satan and the Rebellious Angels" is recited by the faithful followed by a ritual sprinkling of blessed salt and holy water around the property boundary lines to serve as supernatural barriers to those who seek abortions. This is not a formal ritual exorcism which requires a priest exorcist but merely the faithful's recitation of an exorcism prayer against the demons which surround abortion killing centers.

Psalms, canticles, the Divine Mercy Chaplet and the Rosary are also recited at the killing centers together with the singing of many hymns. A special prayer is recited for abortion victims that Our Lady of Guadalupe will help all mothers to reverence and bring forth the life within them and that all abortionists and abortion supporters will be converted. The faithful then recite an Act of Consecration to Our Lady of Guadalupe as Guardians of Life. See Appendices D, G and H for these prayers. Those who are unable to be physically present at the killing centers remain in adoration before the Blessed Sacrament and pray for the intentions of the Guardians of Life.

Many mothers have changed their minds and have turned away from the killing centers in a decision to bring forth the life within them. Several killing centers have been closed after Our Lady's Visitations including centers in Chicago, New Orleans, Santa Fe, and Redwood City, California.

The Missionary Image has been welcomed by many Bishops and several Cardinals. Cardinal James Hickey welcomed her in Washington, D.C. in January of 1992 at a Mass celebrated immediately before the Right to Life March.

Cardinal John Joseph Carberry welcomed her in St. Louis, Missouri in February, 1992 at his retirement home. Cardinal John O'Connor welcomed her in St. Patrick's Cathedral in New York City in October, 1992, preceding a Mass celebrated in reparation for the abominations of Halloween.

Cardinal Roger Mahoney of Los Angeles and Cardinal Jaime Sin of the Philippines welcomed her in Manila, the Philippines during a con-celebrated Mass on the Feast Day of Our Lady of Guadalupe, December 12, 1992. Cardinal Mahoney crowned the Image before two million of the faithful.

Likewise, Archbishop Manuel Castro Ruiz of Merida, Mexico, crowned her in May, 1993 as Queen of the Mexican Youth during the first Mexican Marian Conference in the history of Mexico.

Our Lady is always welcomed by great crowds of the faithful as a Queen and she brings to them a great sense of awe and reverence. She touches the hearts of all those who venerate her. Some cry, some stand in awe, many touch and kiss her and return to their seats only to return again for more veneration. Her presence is felt wherever the Image goes and her children feel a peace which emanates from her that is truly indescribable. Although they know that she is in their hearts, they want to be with her everywhere she goes.

One of the drivers of a van which carried the Image described their Visitation as "probably the most outstanding time of my life. The two predominant emotions of this week's work for Our Lady were fatigue and exhilaration, the latter taking care of the former."

Priests report that they have seen an outpouring of devotion as never seen before. "From the moment I opened the Church at 6:45 a.m., there were groups of people in the Church throughout the day and the all-night vigil until the next morning's Mass. People came from all over the area and further. Confessions were heard from those who had not been in decades. These were days of great graces for our parish and for those who came to express their love for Our Lady."

Almost everyone who venerates her is touched in some way. Some are given an inner strength to deal with their problems and adversities, others receive confirmation of their prayer petitions, others are led to Confession and some are miraculously healed.

A priest reported that several of the faithful travelled along with Our Lady's Image. "Indeed, she captivated many souls. Our Lady said that she would melt hearts and she did just that everywhere she went! Above all, she deeply touched the hearts of the Team members. Each of them wanted to be with her wherever she went. They vied with one another as to who would keep her overnight in their homes. They talked with one another about their individual edifying experiences, both those that they had witnessed and those reported to them by others. . . . In her travels near Dayton, Ohio, Our Lady visited five abortion killing centers, two grade schools totalling over 1,000 students, thirteen parishes, a university chapel, a renewal center and a women's prison. At the prison Our Lady was devoutly and gratefully received by forty of her daughters. They cried, lingered to touch her and told of their childhood memories of the Blessed Mother. They asked for every brochure and Rosary that the Team had brought with them. In all, thousands of brochures, Rosaries, holy cards and medals of Our Lady of Guadalupe were passed out wherever the Image went. Most of these objects were piously touched to the Image.

"The reception and turnout of the faithful for this Visitation were truly gratifying. It far exceeded the expectations of the Team. Love and devotion for Our Lady is abundantly alive. If only the clergy knew how much the laity responds to Our Blessed Mother!"

Another priest said that he spent fourteen hours in the Church and he was awed by the respect and outstanding patience of the pilgrims who venerated the Image on that day. "No one put themselves above others in the long lines. The marvelous quiet and peace in the people gathered together with the number of children was uplifting."

A Guardian reported, "I never imagined the response that Our Lady would receive from the people here, let alone my own response to her. Her presence was deeply experienced as was the Holy Spirit who was almost tangible. It was a day in which heaven truly did touch us and we cherish it. I found myself wanting to protect her and watch over her as I do my own mother, wanting everything to be just as she would want it. She became very real and everything else in my life, including my family, came to a standstill for that time. She captured my heart. My five year old daughter said it best when she said, 'Now we have both Jesus and Mary in our Church.' One is never present without the other but for that day, Mary was physically there with us."

Cloistered nuns have received the Image with great joy. Some exclaimed, "What a grace! We are honored!" It is beautiful to see their joyful faces through the grille as they sing to Our Lady and venerate her. Often times the Image is left with them for their all-night veneration.

A group of Poor Clares greeted her with the cry, "Mother is here!, Mother is here!" They prayed the Rosary and then brought out their guitars as they sang to her. On the wall of the chapel was another image of Our Lady of Guadalupe. With great reverence, the Missionary Image was lifted up to touch this image. A great quiet came over the whole group gathered there as they felt a special blessing had been granted by Our Lady.

When the Guardian Team went out on the street with the Image, they looked at the beautiful sun. "Several of us could see the Host. For a split second there was a dark Cross beside the Host. Then there was a tremendous burst of rose color across the sky and an image of a giant rose-colored monstrance appeared with the Host. The image lasted for several minutes. This image seemed very significant after leaving the Poor Clares since St. Clare is often pictured carrying the monstrance because of her great love for the Eucharist."

Joseyp Terelya, the Ukranian visionary, once carried the Image in procession in Pennsylvania. He said that the image of Our Lady which most resembles his visions of her is Our Lady of Guadalupe.

One of the high points of the Toronto, Ontario Visitation was the Rosary for Life Mass and Walk. With an honor guard of thirty Knights of Columbus, followed by twelve standards bearing the names of the fruits of the Holy Spirit, the Missionary Image was carried in procession. So crowded were the churches that the choir lofts had to be opened to accommodate the overflow. A two and one-half hour penitential Rosary Procession went to all three Toronto abortion killing centers where 700 of the faithful recited the Exorcism Prayer and other prayers as holy water was sprinkled on the grounds of the killing centers.

Another Guardian related that their Visitation of Our Lady was "a time of unprecedented inspiration and joy for me. The veneration filled a need in my life for closer contact with our Blessed Mother and made me realize how many people share the need for God, for the comfort and hope we can receive only by reaching out to a source of aid outside of ourselves, a source of dependence on our Creator and His Blessed Mother to help us through the trials of this life.

"Some may have received miraculous healings. I do know that thousands received Mary's gentle touch to soften their hearts that needed her maternal love. I saw hundreds attend Mass and receive the sacraments of Reconciliation and the Eucharist. I saw them file past the Image by the thousands to touch it, to kiss it, to touch their holy pictures, Rosaries and other religious items to it in the hope that they may carry her touch with them throughout the rest of their lives.

"I saw how she touched them in return, by the tears in their eyes as they walked past the Image, by their devotion as they spoke afterwards about their experiences, and by the renewed faith, hope and consolation that seemed to come into their lives because of their encounter.

"I saw it also after our last Mass when we joined a group of 200 or more pro-lifers across the abortion killing center to pray for the end of abortion. The blizzard-like weather did not deter us as we set the Missionary Image on an easel to face the killing center and prayed our Rosaries for the end of the scourge of abortion."

One Guardian explained the climax of his Visitation with the Image: "We arrived at the Church at 3:00 a.m. to pick up the Image when, to our surprise, the organ started to play. Then a choir started to sing. Suddenly the pastor and curate came out in white vestments for Benediction. At 3:00 a.m.! We were aghast! I looked around and did not see a dry eye.

"At the conclusion of Benediction, the pastor stood and turned to the Image and led us in hymns. Then he approached the Image and knelt in front of it. Bending over forward, he kissed the Image at her feet. The devotion was ended. The weekend had come to its conclusion. These final scenes and the heart-felt devotion enveloped my entire being as I sat in the pew overwhelmed by the experience.

"Finally, we fumbled our way through the directions for packing the case and headed for the airport. On the way there we said a Rosary in thanksgiving for the wonderful blessings and graces we and all the other people have received from the presence of the Missionary Image. This was unquestionably the greatest weekend of my entire life! Everyone was singularly blessed. Those who took an active role were ecstatic with the signs and graces and favors that they received. We all thank Dan Lynch and the Missionary Image apostolate for the privilege of having this wonderful Image of Our Lady of Guadalupe visit us."

Another Guardian poetically wrote that "My mind has not grasped or understood the effects of her visit here - it is beyond words or thoughts. Her touch reaches deep into the heart - the spirit.

"A time on the threshold of heaven - of eternity versus time. Sparks of peace. Love and joy ignited that now burn as longing for God.

"The reality of her - the very essence of her - the Lady of the Triune God - the greatness of her 'littleness' - her transparency that shines with the very love of God.

"A day of days - an immersion - an entry - drawn into by grace. The radiance - the quickening - the love become love.

"We have never seen so many tears and so many melted hearts of the 'children' (of all ages) who came to express their love, to ask forgiveness, to beg for help from the Mother that is ever so gentle, understanding and compassionate. As the sea keeps receiving waters of the rivers that flow into it, so our sweet Mother kept receiving with great kindness these rivers of her children that kept coming to her. She received each and every one and not one of them left untouched or unaware of her motherly love."

As the Missionary Image departed from a convent infirmary, the nuns cried and one said, "Now we know that God has not forgotten us."

At the end of a Visitation to La Guadalupe, Quebec, Canada, a 73 year old visiting nun told the pastor, "I've been a nun for 50 years and this has been the most prayerful weekend of my entire life and I just hope that before I die I have one other weekend like this!"

As the Missionary Image was leaving from Farmington Hill, Michigan, Our Lady said in a private locution, "I will not leave you, my presence will remain." The parishioners obtained another Image of Our Lady of Guadalupe to remind them of her Visitation and her continuing presence.

Italy. In September 1991, a pilgrimage to Italy with the Missionary Image was led by Joan Andrews Bell, a Rescuer missionary to the unborn who spent 2½ years in solitary confinement in a Florida prison; Joe Scheidler, Chicago Pro-Life Activist; and myself. Father Walter Winrich was the spiritual director together with Father Thomas Carleton who is now serving a term of 2½ years in a Massachusetts prison because he would not promise the judge that he would never again rescue the unborn children. We were privileged to have the Missionary Image blessed by Pope John Paul II in a general audience with the pilgrims

We also filed a Canonical Petition with the Holy See to sanction prominent American "Catholic" politicians who support abortion. This was done as an act of charity so that the defendants would be given notice of their errors and an opportunity to repent. It was also done to prevent sacrilege to the Eucharist and scandal to the faithful.

As we bussed throughout Italy, we made a Novena to Our Lady of Sorrows in reparation for the sin of abortion and attended Masses at the Shrines of Maria Goretti, Gerard Majella, Bolsena, Orvietto, Assisi, Loreto, Padre Pio's monastery and St. Michael's Cave.

The Missionary Image was brought into St. Michael's Cave just before Communion. At Communion time some women began to scream like demons. Several fell into a catatonic state and had to be removed from the cave. Many of the congregation began to hiss loudly like snakes. It was as if the demons were protesting the presence of the Missionary Image. It was so bad that the priest had to stop Communion and the Mass and left the altar. The Cave was cleared by the Rector. Then a complete Mass was said with us and the Missionary Image in peaceful reparation. St. Michael is known as the Protector of the Blessed Sacrament and it is believed that he protected it against sacrilege in his cave.

We had public processions with the Missionary Image in the streets of Italy which were accompanied by reverential and tearful local citizens. The pilgrimage turned into a mobile pro-life conference as leaders and pilgrims on the bus gave teachings and witness of their pro-life work and prayed the daily Novena, Rosaries, Divine Mercy Chaplet and Our Lady of Guadalupe's Way of the Cross for the Unborn.

The pilgrimage continued from Italy to Fatima, Portugal. All arrived safely there except for the Missionary Image. As the pilgrims patiently waited for two hours on a bus, the airport was thoroughly searched and the Missionary Image could not be found and no explanation was given for its absence. We ended the pilgrimage without it.

After I arrived home in America, I was inspired while in prayer before the Blessed Sacrament to go to the Basilica Shrine in Mexico City to obtain another replica. Providentially, I was able to meet there with Father Winrich who spoke both English and Spanish and could act as my translator. We obtained another replica image from the Basilica Shrine and proceeded on to Guadalajara where we met with Cardinal Posadas who blessed this as another Missionary Image and composed another prayer for it. He said, "The Catholic people of Mexico and I pray to God that the paths of the Journey of the Missionary Image of Our Lady of Guadalupe throughout the United States of America, become rays of Our Lady's love, care, protection and help for all of her children, particularly the unborn."

We then returned to the Basilica Shrine where we met with Monsignor Schulenburg, the Abbot of the Basilica, who blessed the Missionary Image and signed an Open Letter to the Catholic People of the United States giving the Missionary Image as a gift through him from the Catholic people of Mexico. He prayed, "May the Missionary Image of Our Lady of Guadalupe be a River of Light on her Journey throughout the United States. May she be well received and supported in her mission to end abortion and convert millions of hearts to the Sacred Heart of her Son Jesus and His Holy Church through her Immaculate Heart!"

I then returned to the United States with this new Missionary Image and Our Lady continued on her Journey throughout America through the Local Guardian Teams on her Visitations.

Soon after her Journey was renewed, the original Missionary Image was returned to me by Portugal Airlines without any explanation. Because of these extraordinary circumstances and because of the many requests for me to bring the Missionary Image to other countries and to Marian Conferences, I discerned that Our Lady's plan was for this original Image to be the International Missionary Image while the other Image was to be the National Image for the United States. Since then the International Image has travelled throughout the world and to many Marian Conferences with me while the National Image has continued to travel throughout the United States through the Local Guardian Teams.

Fargo, North Dakota. Fargo, North Dakota has only one abortion killing center in the entire state. This center is operated by a female doctor from Minnesota who flies in to North Dakota to do her killing. In August of 1991, I accompanied the Missionary Image and led a procession to this killing center where the Exorcism Prayer was recited. Afterwards, the Missionary Image was placed in the back of a pick-up truck and driven around the city for all to see. We then proceeded to an old country church on the outskirts of the city which was used for satanic worship. We went to pray against this satanic use. We drove throughout the city and on the highway without any problem but as soon as we approached this building, the Missionary Image flew off the pick-up truck and landed face down on the highway, to our horror! We stopped the truck and I ran back, stopped traffic and picked up the undamaged Image. I replaced her on the truck and we proceeded with more determination. Satan seemed determined to prevent our arrival with the Missionary Image. We entered the old church grounds, recited the Exorcism Prayer, sprinkled holy water on the grounds and left. Soon thereafter the old church was closed up and no evidence of further satanic activity was witnessed.

While I was in Fargo, I visited with Bishop James Sullivan and asked him if he would consider carrying the Blessed Sacrament in a public procession and performing a Benediction at the killing center. He said that he would.

On Sunday, August 16, 1992, I returned with the Missionary Image to Fargo where we led a procession of one thousand of the faithful followed by Bishop Sullivan who carried the Blessed Sacrament in solemn procession to the killing center.

Teenagers carried a banner proclaiming, "TRUTH - teens rescuing unborn tiny humans." "It's something we wanted to do and planned for," said fifteen-year-old Christine Phillips. "Maybe it will help end abortion. I'm happy I'm here."

Bishop Sullivan stood in front of the killing center and said, "We are here today because we have sinned. We can no longer act as innocent bystanders. We cannot stand by and watch the innocent unborn washed out of the womb with saline solution and cut into pieces. We want North Dakota to be a leader so that lives will no longer be taken away in the very spot on which we stand.

"So many people in the last few days have asked me what this is about. Those people just don't know you. Help us, Lord, be followers, perfect Christians, and soldiers of Jesus Christ."

The Bishop then celebrated Benediction in front of the killing center and later led the fifteen decade Rosary and celebrated Mass outdoors at a nearby Carmelite Monastery.

Other Bishops who have accompanied the Missionary Image to killing centers in America are Bishop Donald Montrose in Stockton, California; Bishop Austin Vaughan in Wichita, Kansas; Bishop George Pearce in Rhode Island; and Bishop Andrew McDonald in Little Rock, Arkansas.

After we left Stockton, California in March, 1992, Bishop Montrose addressed all of his priests at the Chrism Mass on Holy Thursday. He said, "A few weeks ago the Missionary Image of Our Lady of Guadalupe was brought into our diocese in order that we might pray that the scourge of abortion would end in our country. Great numbers of our people visited the parishes where the Image was reverenced. Prayers were also recited by the hundreds of people who accompanied the Image to our two killing centers.

"As I visited most of the churches where the Image was being venerated, my conscience bothered me. Although I have always publicly opposed abortion and have been publicly pro-life, I have not taken the active leadership in this cause that I should have taken. My association with Dan Lynch and Inge McNeill, who brought the Missionary Image, was brief but their personal sacrifice and total dedication to this cause made me realize what little I have done. Because I have done very little, as a diocese we have done very little. . . .

"What then are we going to do? As a diocese, I am asking that we undertake a Spiritual Campaign, a campaign of prayer that God will remove this terrible scourge from our diocese. Only he can do it. . . .

"We need a miracle. Let us pray for this miracle. It is a miracle that God would want to give us. If, as a diocese we turn to God with all our hearts, great conversions will take place, and hopefully, the miracle also."

As a part of this Spiritual Campaign, Bishop Montrose distributed cards containing prayers to end abortion, to protect the unborn from abortion, for St. Michael's protection and for Divine Mercy.

Washington, D.C. On January 22, 1992, Cardinal James Hickey welcomed the Missionary Image on behalf of the Archdiocese of Washington, D.C. and celebrated a Mass for the pro-lifers preceding the annual Right to Life March. At the end of the Mass he even sang a song to her and recalled how he had learned it as a young priest on an Indian reservation.

The Archdiocese printed and distributed a holy card of Our Lady of Guadalupe. It contained a prayer which recognized her as the instrument who ended human sacrifice and converted millions in sixteenth century Mexico. It said, "Pray for us now, that we might be God's instruments in ending the holocaust of abortion and euthanasia in our land."

After Mass, the Missionary Image led the Archdiocesan contingent in the Right to Life March. Many people witnessed a blue light in the sun the entire day during the March. At the end of the March, the Missionary Image was placed before the United States Supreme Court and Our Lady reviewed all of the marchers who passed by before her under the Supreme Court's inscription, "Equal Justice Under the Law." However, their "equal justice" is for all except the unborn.

In March of 1992, the National Organization of Women sponsored a march in favor of abortion rights in Washington, D.C. One of the march leaders was Bill Clinton. Eleven of Our Lady's friends and myself placed ourselves and the Missionary Image on the sidewalk at the end of the march route where the marchers would have to make their last turn and pass us before entering into the Mall. We hoped that Our Lady would look upon the marchers and bring them the grace of conversion through our prayers. We had no idea how many people would be in the march as we knelt down to begin our Rosary. As the marchers made their turn and saw the Image, all hell literally broke loose. They screamed blasphemies and insults at the Image and us. They spit and threw condoms at us and the Image and hung coat hangers over my neck. As the parade and the blasphemies continued, we increased our prayers and looked down at the ground rather than at the marchers, some of whom openly flaunted their homosexuality. As we prayed, the feet marched past us in an endless parade which we thought would never end. However, we were supernaturally assisted and were able to kneel on the concrete for three hours and forty-five minutes until the conclusion of the march which included 500,000 marchers. In spite of all of the threats of the marchers, neither we nor the Image was hurt.

In June of 1992, the Missionary Image and myself led a procession of hundreds of the faithful who attended the International Rosary Congress at the National Shrine of the Immaculate Conception. We processed from there to the subway, filled the trains, and continued through the streets towards the United States Supreme Court.

About half-way there, I was stopped by a contingent of policemen who said that I couldn't proceed in a political demonstration and needed a special permit to go to the Supreme Court. I told them that this was a religious procession and not a political demonstration. An officer responded, "Oh yeah, then what is that over there?" as he pointed to the Missionary Image. I said, "It's a religious Image of the Blessed Virgin Mary." He looked at the Missionary Image and, in a complete turn-about, said that he would issue the permit on the spot and that they would help us. Then all the policemen walked into the street blocking the traffic and became Our Lady's personal escorts to and around the Supreme Court and back to the subway station. We processed with the Image around the Supreme Court, recited the Rosary and ended the procession in front of the Court where in unison we all recited with gusto the prayer to St. Michael the Archangel.

As we returned from the Supreme Court, we passed by the monument to Christopher Columbus. Since we were celebrating the 500th anniversary of the evangelization of the Americas, which the American Bishops had entrusted to Our Lady of Guadalupe and since Columbus started it all, we stopped before the monument and prayed through his intercession that God would shed his grace on America in a new evangelization.

On January 21, 1993, the Missionary Image was welcomed at the National Shrine of the Immaculate Conception where she was venerated in an all-night vigil which preceded the annual Right to Life March. The next day, the Image led the entire March just behind the representatives of the hierarchy and again was placed before the Supreme Court where Our Lady reviewed all of the marchers who processed in front of her.

On March 25, 1993, the Feast of the Annunciation, our apostolate sponsored a National Day of Prayer, Fasting and Assembly. All people of good will throughout America were called to join in unison at noon to recite the Angelus in honor of Our Lady who said "Yes" to Life and to recite in unison the Chaplet of Divine Mercy at 3:00 p.m. Eastern Standard time.

Thousands joined us in their local churches and hundreds joined us at the National Shrine of the Immaculate Conception where the Missionary Image and the Image of Jesus King of All Nations were received. After Mass the images led us in procession to the altar of St. Louis de Montfort where we all recited our Act of Total Consecration to the Immaculate Heart of Mary. From there we travelled to Lafayette Park which is located directly opposite the White House. There we recited Rosaries and the Chaplet of Divine Mercy in reparation for the sin of abortion in our land and for the conversion of our government leaders.

Mother Angelica Live. On May 13, 1992, the 75th anniversary of the first apparition of Our Lady of Fatima, I appeared on the Mother Angelica Live television show with the Missionary Image. At one-half hour before showtime the Missionary Image had not arrived. I requested that a back-up image which belonged to Mother Angelica be placed in the studio and this was done. At 20 minutes to showtime, Mother breezed into the makeup room and asked me, "So where's Our Lady, Dan?" I sheepishly replied, "Somewhere between here and Vermont." At 10 minutes to showtime we went to the prayer room to pray for the fruitfulness of the show. Mother prayed fervently for Our Lady's quick arrival. I joined her and prayed to St. Joseph, "There's no time left bring her now!" At that moment a man walked into the room and asked, "Where should the case go?" I asked, "Where is it?" He said, "It's on the floor of the studio." I ran past him into the studio and, before a full studio audience, I fumbled with the lock's combinations and was unable to open them until I took a deep breath and prayed "Help!" Then I calmly opened the case, took out the Image and placed it on the studio stage after the removal of the back-up image. It was one minute to showtime and I victoriously walked towards my seat. But the Image fell down because I misplaced its support pole. I ran back to the stage and anxiously replaced it as the countdown began, "ten, nine, eight, seven, six." I was in my seat at the count of five, took two deep breaths and it was showtime - Mother Angelica Live!

Ireland. A young girl got pregnant in Ireland in 1992 and threatened to commit suicide unless she were allowed to have an abortion in that country where it was illegal. Sinead O'Connor, an Irish rock singer, took to the streets with a few hundred supporters and proclaimed, "We made the law and we can change it." This made world-wide news and providentially I saw it on television.

I sent a fax to Father Gerard McGinnity, spiritual director of Irish visionary Christina Gallagher. I told him that if he could guarantee ten thousand Rosary Processors in Dublin in reparation that I would come with the Missionary Image.

We were invited and in May of 1992, Father Michael O'Carroll, world-reknowned Mariologist, the Missionary Image and myself led a Rosary Procession in Dublin of fifteen thousand of the faithful! This was the largest Rosary Procession in Ireland since the Eucharistic Congress of 1932. We prayed that Ireland would be kept abortion-free.

As we processed, a spray of natural live rose petals fell from the sky in the front ranks of the processors. A similar spray fell upon the speakers' platform at the end of the procession.

During the Visitation, Our Lady of Guadalupe appeared to Christina Gallagher with the stars on her mantle appearing as laser beams of light. Our Lady was pleased with our efforts. Jesus also gave a locution to the Irish mystic Rose O'Reilly on the day of the Rosary Procession: "All the preparation and prayer for this day will not be in vain. Hearts will be touched; souls will be saved; many who would contemplate abortion will not, because of the prayers and efforts of all my little ones. I see your sufferings, I see the confusion, I see the attacks of evil, but remember, dear children, I can crush Satan and all his pomps, but I need the prayers and sufferings of my little ones to offer to my Father."

The next day we travelled with the Missionary Image to Northern Ireland to an outdoor Mass. There Our Lady appeared in the sky to the Irish visionary Beulah Lynch. Beulah said that Our Lady held the child Jesus and He blessed all of us who had gathered around the Image.

As we returned to Ireland with the Image in our van, we must have looked suspicious to the British soldiers at the border. A helicopter flew very low over the van, which blew dirt all around, as if to intimidate us with its noise and presence. It landed just ahead of us at the checkpoint. A British soldier approached us with a machine gun and questioned us very carefully. We explained that our cargo was an image of the Blessed Virgin Mary and we took him to the rear of the van. There we removed the blanket covering the Missionary Image and explained its significance to him. He seemed very moved, so we offered him a replica image to take with him. As he lowered his machine gun, he said, "No thank you, I will take her into my heart." Then he waved us through with a smile.

As the months passed, the movement for abortion rights raged like a forest fire across Ireland fueled by the secular media and government. Finally, the government proposed to the Irish people an amendment to their Constitution, which prohibited abortion, to "legalize" it in certain situations. A referendum vote was scheduled. Once again Our Lady had a special mission.

We were called to come to Ireland again in November of 1992. This time we made many Visitations to many churches to pray and fast against legalized abortion in Ireland. For ten days we called upon the Irish martyrs to intercede to save Ireland from the abortion threat and the secular enemy within which was far greater than the British enemy in the past.

I had a desire to climb Croagh Patrick. Croagh Patrick is St. Patrick's mountain on the west coast of Ireland. It has been a mountain of penance for over 1,500 years. St. Patrick himself prayed and fasted on its summit for forty days during his Lenten fast. He prayed that Ireland would preserve the faith until the end of time. I expressed a desire to Eammon O'Connor, our Irish host, to imitate St. Patrick and to make a climb in reparation for those who wanted "legalized" abortion in Ireland. He said that due to the unpredictable and severe weather changes in late Fall, "Only American idiots climb Croagh Patrick in November!" I said, "Okay, that's me, let's go!" So Eammon, my wife Sue, another lady and myself made the arduous climb to the top without incident.

As we climbed, we prayed at various stations along the way. The last station was the summit. As we approached the summit on our hands and knees because of the small, slippery shale pieces on the surface, the sky darkened and clouds quickly moved in from the Atlantic Ocean. Soon we were in the midst of a major hail storm and couldn't see more than fifty yards ahead of us nor the trail back. It was as if Satan did not want us to complete the last of St. Patrick's stations. Nevertheless, we triumphantly marched around the summit of the mountain and completed our prayers. Slowly and carefully we began our descent, although we couldn't see the trail. Suddenly a tunnel of light approximately two hundred yards wide appeared over the trail and led us safely down the mountain! We gave thanks to Our Lady.

Our Irish pilgrimage ended at Knock Shrine which was filled with six thousand of the faithful on a beautiful Spring-like day. It was very unusual to have such fine weather so late in the Fall which is out-of-season for the Shrine. It was so nice out that we had our closing Rosary Procession outside on the Shrine grounds. Father Michael O'Carroll preached to the congregation followed by a talk by myself. I exhorted the Irish people to be true to the faith in imitation of the Irish martyrs who were beatified by Pope John Paul II and to follow his teaching that no one may vote to "legalize" abortion under any circumstances. I said, "As they died for their faith, let us *live* ours!"

During the Mass, Our Lady of Guadalupe appeared from the Missionary Image and looked from side to side throughout the Shrine smiling with approval on the faithful gathered there. This was witnessed by the mother of the driver of the van which transported the Image. This witness was a very refined and stable lady who was wondering why her daughter, appropriately named Mary, a registered nurse, was wasting her time driving this Image all over Ireland. Now she knew that Our Lady was giving her seal of approval.

Before the Missionary Image arrived in Ireland, the polls said that 70% of the Irish people favored "legalized" abortion. After the Visitation, the polls changed to 70% *against* "legalized" abortion and soon thereafter the proposed Constitutional amendment to "legalize" abortion was defeated by the Irish people. This victory has been attributed to Our Lady of Guadalupe by the Irish faithful.

Victorious Queen of the World Peace Flight. In October of 1992, the Missionary Image and myself led large processions in Lourdes, France and Fatima, Portugal as part of the World Peace Flight pilgrimage of over one thousand pilgrims, six bishops and sixty priests and six tons of religious goods for Russia. The pilgrimage was organized by Rosalie Turton of the 101 Foundation.

On October 13, 1992, the 75th anniversary of the last apparition of Fatima, the Missionary Image and the Image of Jesus King of All Nations were placed in the middle of the Fatima plaza which was filled with approximately a half million pilgrims.

Our Lady had prophesied through Jane Garza (an American visionary) a Filipino visionary and a priest, all of whom were on our pilgrimage, that she would send a dove at Fatima as a sign for us to have confidence in her intercession. Sure enough, after the Mass a dove came down from the sky and alighted above the left hand of the Image of Jesus King of All Nations. It reminded us of what John the Baptist said, "I saw the Spirit descend from the sky like a dove and remain upon Him." Jn 1:32.

Another visionary reported that at that moment rays appeared from the Missionary Image glowing out in all directions onto the crowd and Our Lady was smiling from her Image upon all her people. This woman reported that "During the time that I was having this inner vision I think a bomb could have dropped in front of me and I would not have been able to move because the vision was so intense." The Filipino visionary also saw Our Lady of Guadalupe come from her Image and bright light proceed from her to the crowd. Our Lady then appeared to Jane Garza and said, "I am the Lady of Light and I will enlighten each one of you."

On this day, a historic live television broadcast was made of the proceedings at Fatima to 40 million people of the former Soviet Union. Archbishop Kondrusiewicz of Moscow and the Bishop of Fatima unreservedly implored Our Lady's blessing and protection for Russia.

Three days later, on our way to Russia, Our Lady of Guadalupe appeared to Jane Garza and said, "Do not have the smallest worry. You should only be concerned with being in a loving and prayerful spirit."

As we entered Moscow, our tour guide said that she was happy to welcome us to the city and pleased to say that it was now the capital of *Russia* and no longer of the Soviet Union. She said, "Although we had seventy-three years of atheism and were brought up as atheists, yet we were born with the love of God in our hearts, and we really are true Christians and we welcome you to pray with us. I welcome you with an open heart and tears in my eyes and we thank you for coming. Like the universe we are not separated anymore. We are not closed anymore. We are allowed to tell you what we feel and we are happy about this so that when you come here to share with us all of our troubles you can join us in looking to the future with optimism. Because as long as you are with us and we are all together as children of God, it makes us happy.

"Our young people have no morals because they were brought up through atheistic Communism and there was no model of goodness for them. There were no parents, no teachers, no persons to tell them the difference between right and wrong. There was no one. But now they must learn that even if there is no one, they are not alone here and that there is always God with them who loves them and who will help them to do good. Thank you for praying for Russia. This is what we need. You have brought love to this country, you have brought us God. Thank you."

We distributed 6 tons of religious goods and ten thousand holy cards of Our Lady of Guadalupe which contained the prayer set forth in Appendix I. These holy cards were gratefully received by the Russian people who often read them with tears in their eyes as soon as they received them. None were thrown to the ground as often happens elsewhere.

On October 18, as we approached Red Square in Moscow on our bus, I led the Visitation mystery of the Rosary. As I meditated, I told the pilgrims that I was sorry that we had not planned a big pageant for Our Lady to triumphantly enter Red Square like Jesus entered Jerusalem to the waving of palm leaves and the sound of Hosannahs. "Then again," I said, "it's the little unplanned things that hit our Mother's heart such as when a six year old gives a scribbly birthday card to her mother, as compared to when a 21 year old gives an embroidered tablecloth. So let's just offer our Mother our scribbles today as her little children in her motley army."

As we reached Red Square, we got the Missionary Image and the Image of Jesus King of All Nations out from the bus together with a large cross and, as we sang "Onward Christian Soldiers," I led a procession to the edge of Red Square which was barricaded. We waited outside the barricades in front of the site of the former Cathedral of Kazan, which had been destroyed by Stalin, for the arrival of the International Pilgrim Virgin statue of Our Lady of Fatima. As I looked across the immense plaza of Red Square, I could see some of our blue-coated pilgrims on the other side. One of our priests said that the Pilgrim Virgin statue was across the Square and he opened the barricade a little bit. I told the pilgrims to follow me and to break through the barricades as I led the images with the cross across Red Square and approached the other side. The Russian police were astonished that we passed the barricades but our priest calmed their fears and they let us proceed.

Many of us pilgrims saw the Pilgrim Virgin statue on the other side of the Square being carried high above the heads of the people gathered there. So we processed towards her. In fact, what we saw was an apparition of the statue and not the statue itself, which never entered Red Square that morning. Our Lady used this apparition to draw me and the pilgrims across the entire length of Red Square towards St. Basil's Cathedral on the other side. As I approached St. Basil's, the apparition disappeared and I had no idea where to go.

Out of the corner of my eye I saw a circular platform monument with nine concrete steps. I literally ran to the top of these steps urging everyone to follow me and to surround me and the images so that the police would not arrest us. I planted the cross at the top of the platform in a manner reminiscent of the Marines planting the flag on the top of Mt. Surabachi on Iwo Jima.

Here I proclaimed Our Lady as Queen of Russia and of All Nations and Jesus as King of Russia and All Nations. I said that we were there to claim the country of Russia for the Immaculate Heart of Mary and Christ the King. I said, "When the Holy Father consecrated Russia and the world to the Immaculate Heart of Mary in 1984, Sister Lucia said that God will keep His promise, meaning that Russia will be converted." I continued, "The conversion of Russia will ignite the Divine Flame of the love of God which will proceed from Russia throughout the entire world and set the whole world on fire for Christ so that Jesus Christ will be truly King of All Nations and will reign in all hearts."

John Haffert, founder of the Blue Army, was standing next to me. I handed him a tiny crown from a small statue of Our

Lady of Fatima held by pilgrim Janice Flynn. I announced that Our Lady was so humble that she came in this small statue, rather than the International Pilgrim Virgin statue, and I said to John, "In honor of your forty plus years of service to Our Lady please crown her as Queen of Russia." He did so.

At that moment, Jane Garza said that Red Square lit up like the Fourth of July in a vision that she had. Our Lady appeared to her and said that she was very pleased and happy with all of our efforts and troubles. She appeared as Our Lady of Fatima over Red Square wearing a crown. Light streamed from her heart flooding the Square and bounced up and outwards in all directions. She said: "Thank you for your obedience and prayers. You, my children, have overcome many obstacles by obedience and prayer. You have brought so much joy to my heart. Know that your rewards are great in heaven for you have pleased God. Remain small in the eyes of the world so that you may be great in the eyes of God.

"Your sister Russia, my children, needs your love and faith. My children, I too am embracing my children in Russia. Let us go together and embrace her with God's love."

Later, our tour guide told me that she was astonished that we were able to process into Red Square without being stopped by the police. She added that the spot from which I proclaimed the Queenship and Kingship of Mary and Jesus was a monument from which the Tsars used to proclaim their edicts to the Russian peoples and that I made the proclamation in front of Spasskey Tower on the Kremlin Wall which means "Savior's Tower."

The Philippines. In December of 1992, the Missionary Image was venerated by thousands upon thousands of Filipinos as it toured throughout the Philippine Islands on a mission to keep that country free from international agencies which sponsor so-called population control programs which promote the use of artificial contraceptives.

The Missionary Image and myself were received by President Fidel Ramos, the vice president and the entire cabinet at the Filipino "White House" where a Mass was celebrated in honor of Our Lady of Guadalupe. Prior to the Mass I personally addressed President Ramos and said: "Mr. President I am the Ambassador of Our Lady of Guadalupe and I beg you on her behalf not to implement any so-called population control programs which promote the use of artificial contraceptives." He responded, "We don't have any population-control programs we only have population-management programs." I could see already that the euphanisms had affected his judgment, as if by his calling it "management" it made it moral regardless of the means employed.

On the Feast Day of Our Lady of Guadalupe, a Mass was con-celebrated in Luneta Park, Manila by Filipino Cardinal Jaime Sin and Cardinal Roger Mahoney of Los Angeles, together with twelve bishops and sixty priests. Cardinal Mahoney was designated by Pope John Paul II as his personal representative. The Mass was celebrated before President Ramos, former President Coryzon Aquino and two million Filipino faithful.

They honored the Missionary Image and Cardinal Mahoney crowned her as the Patroness of the Philippine Islands as she had been proclaimed by Pope Pius XI.

I exhorted the faithful to resist efforts of international Freemasonry to bring to the Philippines so-called "population control" programs of artificial contraception which had led to worldwide abortion. I urged them "to reject so-called 'safe sex' and to practice 'sacred sex', only within marriage and always open to the transmission of new life."

Over seventy beautiful images of the Blessed Mother from all over the Philippines were escorted by the faithful in a regal procession of several miles to the Luneta grandstand.

The Mass was followed by a candlelight ceremony while we sang "The Light of Christ" as a symbol and hope for reverence for life, peace and unity in the Philippines and the rest of the world. The entire celebration was broadcast over national Filipino television and seen by millions.

Our Lady of Guadalupe said in her recent messages that "I want millions to see my Image, the Woman Clothed with the Sun." See Appendix A, Second Message. This message has been literally fulfilled through her television appearances in the Philippines, Ireland, and America.

The Missionary Image has also been venerated by tens of thousands at Marian Conferences in Baltimore; Chicago; Cleveland; Denver; Des Moines; Kansas City; Minneapolis; New Orleans; New York City; Notre Dame; Pittsburgh; Portland; Pueblo, Colorado; St. Louis; St. Paul; San Diego; San Francisco; Santa Maria, California; Spokane; Tulsa; Washington, D.C.; Wichita; Worcester, Massachusetts and many other cities.

Audrey Santo. Audrey is an eight year old girl victim soul who lives in Worcester, Massachusetts. She is in a semi-coma and requires 24-hour nursing care in her home from her devoted mother, grandmother and others. They monitor her breathing and keep her tracheotomy clear. Audrey became comatose after she nearly drowned in her grandmother's swimming pool when she was three years old on August 9, 1987 at 11:03 a.m., the precise date and time when the first atomic bomb was dropped on Nagasaki, Japan in 1945. Perhaps her suffering is saving us from nuclear war. Before her accident, Audrey used to go to daily Mass with her grandmother.

In 1988, her mother took her on a difficult pilgrimage to Medjugorje, Yugoslavia hoping for a miraculous healing. Audrey was brought to the balcony where Our Lady's apparitions took place. She appeared very lively during the apparition, as if she too was seeing the Blessed Mother. Audrey seemingly shook her head "yes" and then fell into cardiac arrest and almost died. It is believed that Audrey actually did see the Blessed Mother during the apparition and that she was given a choice to be healed or to accept her suffering as a victim soul. Audrey apparently chose the latter.

Because she was critically ill, no commercial airliner would take Audrey home because of the possibility of her death during the flight. Her mother had to incur thousands of dollars to hire the United States military to fly her home. Later Audrey manifested the stigmata. Her only solid food is the daily Eucharist. Many souls are being saved by her victimhood.

The Missionary Image has made two Visitations to Audrey Santo's home. One Visitation had a large gathering of people who attended a Mass celebrated by a Bishop. The other Visitation was private.

On the first visit the Image stayed with Audrey overnight in her bedroom. On the second visit, her mother told me that Audrey was probably able to hear and see within a few inches of her face. So I stuck my face in hers and said, "Audrey, I love you! Your mother said that you can probably see and hear within a few inches of your face so take a good look at *this* face and pray for me and my guardianship of the Missionary Image and all of her Visitations. Please offer all of your suffering for this apostolate." A tear fell from her eye which her mother later said is a sign that she understood me. Since then Audrey Santo has been the victim soul for the Missionary Image apostolate.

A visionary visited Audrey at her home and while in her bedroom had a vision of Our Lady of Guadalupe all dressed in white. Audrey's grandmother then opened her eyes widely and exclaimed, "I see her! I see her!"

Image Crownings. The Missionary Image was crowned "Queen of the World Youth" by Bishop Roman Danylak of Toronto, Canada during the only Marian Forum at World Youth Day 1993 in Denver, Colorado. Bishop Danylak placed the world youth under the protective mantle of Our Lady of Guadalupe.

This crowning had been prefigured in Merida, Mexico which the Pope visited on his way to Denver. In May at Merida, during the first Mexican Marian Conference, Archbishop Ruiz crowned the Missionary Image "Queen of the Mexican Youth." The Missionary Image has also been crowned as Queen of International Youth 2000 in London, England and National Youth 2000 in Chicago, Illinois.

Missionary Image in a beautiful display.

Ready to travel with the Missionary Image and Guardian Lorraine Rodriguez (right) during the New Mexico Visitation.

Our Lady's Guadalupana musicians who accompanied the Missionary Image throughout New Mexico and Colorado. Note Our Lady's tee shirts.

St. Michael's Cave, Gargano, Italy. From right Joe Scheidler, Chicago pro-life activist; Joan Andrews Bell, rescuer-victim for the unborn, and author.

Bishop James Sullivan carrying Blessed Sacrament in public procession of 1,000 faithful to Fargo, North Dakota abortion killing center where he conducted Benediction.

Missionary Image on steps of United States Supreme Court which "legalized" abortion. Note words inscribed across the Court's facade, "Equal Justice Under Law" - for all except the unborn.

World renowned Mariologist, Father Michael O'Carroll and author leading a Rosary Procession of 15,000 faithful in Dublin, Ireland in reparation for abortion.

Irish visionary Christina Gallagher with Missionary Image.

Author at the summit of Croagh Patrick (St. Patrick's Mountain), Ireland which was climbed in reparation for abortion.

Fatima, Portugal on the 75th anniversary of Our Lady's last apparition there, October 13, 1992, with the Missionary Image and the image of Jesus King of All Nations upon which a dove landed and remained as prophesied by three mystics.

Victorious Queen of the World Peace Flight pilgrims (Our Lady's airborne Blue Army) in front of the Church at Lourdes, France.

Author leading a procession of the image of Jesus King of All Nations, the Missionary Image and Victorious Queen of Peace pilgrims into Red Square, Moscow, Russia on October 18, 1992.

Author proclaiming Our Lady as Queen and Jesus as King of Russia and All Nations in Red Square after crowning of small statue of Our Lady of Fatima by Blue Army founder John Haffert.

From right, Inge McNeill co-ordinator of Missionary Image apostolate; June Keithley Castro, Director of the Center of Peace for Asia; and author in front of 2 million Filipino faithful in Luneta Park, Manila, Philippines, on the Feast Day of Our Lady of Guadalupe, December 12, 1992.

Missionary Image looking over Audrey Santo, victim-soul of the apostolate.

16. Signs, Wonders and Conversions

Signs and Wonders. Many signs and wonders have been performed on Our Lady's Journey. When the first Missionary Image left Mexico City for Central America at noon on June 9, 1991, a solar phenomenon occurred which was witnessed by millions. It was reported on television and on the front page of newspapers. The sun appeared as a brilliant host visible to the naked eye. It was surrounded by a blue aureola cloud which in turn was surrounded by a round rainbow. It was in this manner that Our Lady of Guadalupe first appeared to Juan Diego on December 9, 1531 and emerged to him from the brilliant light. She is the Woman Clothed with the Sun. See Rev 12:1.

The photograph of this phenomenon reveals trees on the bottom right which shows that the sun was unusually low for high noon. It also shows a young woman on the bottom left looking directly at the sun. The large blue aureola cloud caused it to be very dark in the middle of the day. This darkness further elucidated the bright sun which was covered by an opaque white disc which enabled people to look directly at it.

This phenomenon was explained in the media as "probably caused by a reflection of the King Asteroid through particles of ice in the atmosphere at a great height from the earth."

However, those with faith know that the true King of kings gave this sign because His Mother is a reflection of Himself.

This very same solar sign was witnessed by many in appropriately named Sunnyvale, California. As we were peacefully praying the Rosary at an abortion killing center, this sign appeared in the sky. We fell to our knees in awe. A priest witness testified that the sun in the middle of the aureola cloud spun magnificently and moved throughout the cloud, even disappearing at times!

On July 30, 1991, two Polaroid photographs were taken of the Missionary Image in a darkened church at night in Burlington, Vermont. One photograph was dark, the other revealed an apparent cloud of fire hovering over the Image as shown on the front cover of this book. This is reminiscent of the cloud of fire which covered the Ark of the Covenant at night. See Nm 9:15-16; Ex 40:38. Our Lady is the Ark of the New Covenant since, as the pregnant Mother of Jesus, she carried the presence of God as did the original Ark. This photograph was placed on the cover of the Missionary Image apostolate's explanatory brochure and has been distributed throughout the world.

When we were in Ireland on November 11, 1992, the very first day of the Visitation, the Image was placed for veneration in an Oratory which was located in a commercial shopping mall. One of the shoppers came in out of curiosity. She was a Protestant and didn't know anything about Our Lady of Guadalupe. She was alone with the Image.

Then one of the Guardian Team came into the Oratory with some of our brochures. The woman saw the cover photograph of the cloud of fire and excitedly testified that she had just witnessed the entire Oratory fill with this very same cloud of fire as she prayed for reconciliation and unity of the churches.

At the first Visitation of the Missionary Image at the International Rosary Congress in Washington, D.C. in June 1991, a group of fifty venerators saw "as if in a dream" Our Lady appear from the Image and hold out the crowned Child Jesus. Two fetuses appeared on her womb. These could represent the physical Body of Christ and the Mystical Body of Christ, the Church, as Our Lady is the Mother of both of them.

On the Feast day of Our Lady of Guadalupe, December 12, 1991, the Guardian Team was transporting the Image in a motor home in New Mexico. A group of us were sitting at a table near the rear window. It had been a cloudy, dreary day but the sun was just beginning to peek through the clouds into the rear window. Suddenly, I looked to the sun and teasingly prayed, "Jesus, shine forth on your Mother's Day!" Immediately, the sun enlarged, shined brilliantly, "blinked" like a great traffic light in the sky and spun to the awe of everyone!

Hundreds of people have witnessed the so-called "Miracle of the Sun" over the Missionary Image. Most often this occurs upon its arrival for a Visitation and when placed in front of abortion killing centers. The sun spins wildly in the sky, showing forth a rainbow of colors and different holy images. It pulsates and radiates light and is visible for long periods with the naked eye.

One night in January, 1992, we were in Herndon, Virginia. The Image was placed for veneration in a private home. We were going to take it to Georgetown University to pray in reparation for the activity that was permitted there by homosexual advocates.

I went out to my van to get something and as I returned to the house I noticed a beautiful full moon which was low on the horizon. We then carried the Missionary Image from the house towards the van. As we did so, the moon began to rise from the horizon. Eight of us saw the moon rise and rapidly come across the sky, like a satellite, finally coming to rest directly over the Image which we had placed in the middle of the street!

In their reverential devotion, many of the faithful touch and kiss the Missionary Image. In doing so, many have felt warmth, an electric-like current, and even Our Lady's heartbeat and a womb of flesh, beneath which they felt the movement and kicking of an unborn child. Others have seen fetuses in the womb. One mother went so far as to listen to Our Lady's womb with a stethoscope. She clearly heard a heartbeat and the sounds of movement of a fetus in amniotic fluid!

Here's how one woman described her "touch" at the Denver Marian Conference in December 1992. "I waited in line for prayer before the Image. It was as though Our Lady beckoned me to place my hand upon her womb. In my hand was my Rosary from San Vittorino that Our Lady's presence turned to gold on Mount Podbrodo in Medjugorje.

"Immediately I felt a strong heat and then the pulsing of the very heartbeat of Jesus. There was only one heartbeat, as Our Lady and Our Lord's hearts beat as one for all mankind. The pulsing penetrated my hand and flowed through my arm. My initial interior response was, 'What's happening?' This was not important to know, but that I was to intercede.

"Our Lady said to my heart, 'Pray for every woman now who is even contemplating having an abortion in the United States . . . in the world.' I was very warm, but it was not uncomfortable, rather comforting. The Missionary Image is a Living Image of Our Lady, a perpetual apparition, hidden under the appearance of the veiled Image of Guadalupe."

Many have smelled an overwhelming aroma of roses in the presence of the Missionary Image. The aroma is unmistakeable and cannot be attributed to any other source.

Some have seen tears in Our Lady's eyes and on her cheeks. This happened at the first Marian Conference where the Image was venerated in Pueblo, Colorado. A man saw a tear fall from her eye and the Lord told him to touch it. He did and oil adhered to his finger. Later at home he blessed his mother with the same finger and she felt an electric-like shock go through her body from head to toe.

Many have seen the Missionary Image radiate brilliant light, turn into gold light and appear three dimensional. At the Shrine of Our Lady of Consolation in Carey, Ohio in December 1992, at least five people witnessed brilliant diamond-like light radiating from the tassel over Our Lady's womb. This same light was witnessed over a Franciscan Brother who had arranged the day. It was reported that "on that day so many Rosaries were prayed and Sacraments received that Our Lady must have been radiantly happy and sent one of her rays of love over the Brother who had spent so much of his time and energy receiving the Image and her venerators. We thank God for the precious gift of His Mother who uses days like this to draw us closer and closer to her Son."

At the Spokane Marian Conference in May 1992, a witness reported that "this Image is truly alive and breathing! How strongly we smelled the aroma of roses which emanated from her! Our Lady came to life in three dimension and made slow, graceful movements. Her head moved from side to side and her clothes swayed gently as though in a soft breeze. Her face was beautiful and full of love. A brilliant white light also radiated from her heart and her womb. It was a beautiful sight!"

At Silver Spring, Maryland in February, 1993, five people were in a church on the day of the arrival of the Missionary Image. In front of the altar they saw an oval of light with a figure that looked like Our Lady of Guadalupe. Light from this oval illuminated the first three pews of the church. Another figure appeared in red. Both figures were moving. Our Lady appeared to be beckoning the witnesses to come. They all felt instinctively that the figure in red was Padre Pio who was apparently celebrating Mass in preparation for the Visitation of the Image.

Some people have had interior visions of Our Lady appearing from the Missionary Image. In New Mexico in December, 1991 a very sick Indian woman had a vision of a large case being loaded at an angle in the back of a small white pickup truck with a blue stripe on its side. Our Lady of Guadalupe arose and came from within the case and instantly healed her.

Later she came to the home of the Guardian as we arrived there with the Image packed in a case and loaded at an angle on the back of a pickup truck exactly as it all appeared in her vision!

At the Pueblo, Colorado Marian Conference in October 1991, several children fell and rested in the Spirit as they venerated the Missionary Image. At the New Orleans Marian Conference in December 1991, a teenage venerator fell to the floor "like a sack of quarters dropped from waist high." Everyone was concerned that she was seriously injured but she arose about seven minutes later unharmed and, still in a daze, said that she felt clean and purified. Similarly, at the Tulsa Marian Conference in June 1992, a nun fell to the floor with a loud thud even before she reached the Image. She arose later without harm.

At the Worcester, Massachusetts Marian Conference in May of 1992, the Missionary Image was attacked by a man who was apparently under the influence of drugs. As he raised his fist to strike her in front of six witnesses, he was supernaturally thrown into the air six feet backwards and landed with a thud on his back. After some time he recovered and staggered away as the witnesses continued their Rosary. They reported that the attacker's arm "shot back as if he received an electric shock and he bounced off the ground and lay as if dead!"

Many of the signs and wonders which accompany the Missionary Image have been associated with the abortion holocaust. At Boulder, Colorado, the Image shed tears at a late-term abortion killing center on December 28, 1991, the Feast of the Holy Innocents. The Image was being processed in front of this killing center while the Rosary was prayed. Suddenly, tears began to flow from the right eye down to the center of the right cuff. The tears left a shiny residue which was readily visible. This phenomenon was repeated later that day when the Image was venerated in a private home.

A witness said, "Think of the pain that it took to wrench these tears from our Mother's eye. I felt like crying because Mary was feeling such pain. I wish that I could erase such hurt from her. As a witness to these tears I have a new ache in my heart that seems to be piercing my gut. Intellectually, I knew that Mary suffered greatly for our ungodly ways, selfish hearts and the cruel killing of the unborn, but after witnessing her tears I feel a deeper understanding. Dear Jesus, have mercy on us for our brutality. Your message was one of love and forgiveness and we are totally ignoring it! How your heart must bleed! I am so sorry."

At Wichita, Kansas on August 25, 1991, the Missionary Image shed rose petals. This was also at a late-term abortion killing center. Here the dead bodies are cremated in an incinerator located on the premises. As the Image was processed around the killing center, many smelled an overwhelming aroma of roses. Soon rose petals were seen falling from the Image.

An eyewitness picked up a petal which, she said, "was the most peaceful experience that I've ever had. It was as if the Blessed Mother was saying to me, 'It's good for you to be here. I understand the grief that you feel here at the site of the killing. I know the pain that you feel. Remember that I stood at the foot of the Cross and watched people unjustly kill my innocent Son. I am with you!' Our Lady gave me the strength and the peace to be there. I couldn't stop crying. I was just overcome. I felt that heaven had come down to earth!"

Many witnesses have smelled the roses at abortion killing centers, have heard angelic music and have seen the "Miracle of the Sun" and even a path of gold in front of the processed Image!

In South Hadley, Massachusetts on January 10, 1991, the Missionary Image was taken on an area-wide all-night ride in a van with adult and children occupants who prayed in front of many abortion killing centers.

The next morning they noticed the "Miracle of the Sun" and pulled the van to the side of the road to watch it. To their astonishment black balls came from the sun and formed into fetuses. A witness gasped, "These must be the unborn babies that we saved from abortion through our prayers during the night." Hundreds of these fetus-balls came directly towards the van. As they approached, they turned into green heart-shapes with bright blue circles in the middle. They came through the trees, across the highway and "danced" over the passing cars. The witnesses were crying with excitement and yelled, "They're coming into the van! They're coming into the van!"

As they entered the van, they turned into an indescribable kelly green color and suddenly converged before their very eyes and formed the letter "M" in exquisite calligraphy approximately three feet high which filled the van from ceiling to floor! The color green stands for hope and life and the letter "M" is Our Lady's own personal signature!

At Sunnyvale, California in July, 1992 many witnessed the solar phenomenon of the sun encircled by a blue aureola cloud and a round rainbow. As the witnesses galked at this, another witness looked down at the sidewalk and saw a fresh heel print embedded in the concrete with a sole print which appeared like the rays which surround Our Lady of Guadalupe. As others began to view this footprint, they began to express doubts about its miraculous appearance. As they did so, another footprint exactly the same appeared before their eyes! This heel reminds us of the promise that Our Lady's lowly heel will crush the proud head of Satan. See Gn 3:15.

This is the victory for which we wait in joyful hope. In the meantime, Our Lady gives us these signs and wonders in order to build up our hope and confidence in her heavenly intercession. At least four abortion killing centers have closed after a Visitation of the Missionary Image and Our Lady's prayer supporters in Chicago, New Orleans, Santa Fe, and Redwood City, California.

As the faithful venerate the Missionary Image they answer Our Lady's request to "be free to move about among my children so that they may see me, their Mother, and come to me for comfort and help in these dark and dangerous times." See Appendix A, First Message. As her children do so, she brings them to Eucharistic Adoration as she always leads to her Son Jesus.

In the Grotto Sanctuary of Our Sorrowful Mother in Portland, Oregon on August 15, 1991, the Feast of the Assumption, a photograph was taken of the Missionary Image which reveals a shape of the Eucharist above her finger tips. There was no natural explanation for this photograph nor another one which shows the Eucharist to the left of Our Lady's head.

Many healings have occurred in the presence of the Missionary Image. As a three year old little girl lay dying of cancer in a hospital in Louisville, Kentucky, the Image was brought to visit her. She was healed instantaneously. In the Philippines a man who had been crippled for years rose from his wheelchair as he touched the Image. In Texas a woman who hadn't walked in nine years processed behind the Image for two miles. Also in Texas, a four year old autistic boy who had never spoken, held the Image and said, "Mary I love you, Mary I love you!" He's still talking.

One Guardian was a mother who had prayed for years for her son's healing from alcoholism. On the day of the Visitation, she was injured and unable to welcome the Image in her home. Her son did so and as the Image arrived he said, "Mary, I'm sorry that my mother couldn't welcome you." He clearly heard Our Lady say, "I didn't come here for your mother, I came for you!" He hasn't had a drink since.

At the Baltimore Marian Conference in September, 1992, a woman prayed before the Image for her niece who had developed a rare disease of the hands during her pregnancy so that she was unable to hold her newborn child. The woman said that "Our Lady, who became a very young mother, understood her suffering and she answered my prayers. Now my niece can do anything that a mother should do for her baby."

Conversions. The presence of the Missionary Image has also brought many conversions in answer to Our Lady's promise to melt hearts. Men have cried like babies before the Image.

At a prison in Asheville, North Carolina on November 2, 1992, the Image was venerated by an embarrassed group of prisoners who were reacting to peer pressure. As the Image was leaving, a prisoner yelled to the Guardian Team, "Wait!" The Team stopped, turned and watched a big, handsome, young man walk up to the Image, place a prayer card on Our Lady's heart and say, "Mary, I love you!"

At the last Mass in Charlotte, North Carolina, a woman was seen entering the vestibule sobbing. She said that she had prayed in front of the Image for her agnostic husband's conversion, consecrated him to Our Lady of Guadalupe and was overjoyed to see him just then walk into the Church!

A skeptic went to see the Missionary Image in Meadsville, Pennsylvania. He saw the faithful touching the Image with their prayer petitions and religious articles. This "turned him off."

He said, "My mother and cousin both tried to get me to go up to the Image but I wasn't ready. I just wanted to look. My mother left me and proceeded up to the Image. The next thing I knew, my body became very warm, numb and I fell back against the pew and tried to fight it and remain normal. But I was fighting something more powerful than myself. I fell to my knees and began to cry instantly. I felt so good that I didn't know why I was crying. I didn't want it to end. I knew it was really happening but I didn't really believe in these signs. It made me feel special and proved to me that God still loved me. It also said to me that I better straighten out and serve God first. I realize that there will be many more trials and tribulations but I will always remember the day that God chose to touch me through His Mother!"

Another skeptic in Meadsville who was a recent convert from Protestantism witnessed Our Lady smiling from the Image upon his wife who was also a recent convert. He said, "As a new Catholic I retained a great deal of skepticism about religious objects like the Missionary Image and even more so about the Rosary and the Blessed Mother. Despite my reservations, I accompanied my wife to see the Image because she had such a heartfelt desire to see it. I even knelt in front of the Image and prayed the Rosary. As I prayed I was amazed at the warmth which seemingly radiated from the Image. It was like kneeling in front of a glowing fire on a winter's night. As I knelt, I watched my wife pray earnestly and I hoped that she would experience what I had felt. I looked up to the Image and saw that Our Lady's eyes looked directly at my wife who was praying in front of her. As I watched, Our Lady's facial expression changed and I clearly saw her smile upon my wife! Several times I looked away to find a "rational" explanation but each time that I looked back, the smile remained!"

Our Lady has melted hearts and reconciled enemies through her Image. Three New Mexican Indian chiefs who had been fighting with each other for years came to the Mass which celebrated her Feast Day on December 12, 1991. They sat side by side in prayer in front of the Image. This was a powerful sign to their people of unity and Our Lady's gift of peaceful reconciliation.

Through her Image, Our Lady has melted the hearts of many mothers at abortion killing centers and they have changed their minds and decided to bring forth new life.

We took the Image to a cemetery in Chicago, Illinois in February, 1992. Our Lady was reportedly appearing there. I placed the Image at the foot of a large outdoor Cross and was praying silently before speaking. Vicki, a young pregnant mother, who was scheduled to have an abortion, came by with her mother to hear the visionary speak. She looked at the Image, her knees began to shake and she began to cry. She was not familiar with Our Lady of Guadalupe or the significance of the Image. As she looked at the Image, she felt as if an interior voice said to her, "You are called to motherhood." Immediately she decided to keep her baby.

Just then I began to speak about Our Lady being our "fountain of life" and for life. Her mother turned to her and apologized for exposing her to this talk. Her daughter replied, "It's all right Mom, I've decided to keep the baby."

The pregnant mother then expressed her needs to one of the venerators. She had no money or help. This was passed on to a local parish and they decided to "adopt" mother and baby! The parish announced that they would support the mother with prayer, encouragement and financial gifts whenever possible. They said, "We will experience with her the fears and worries as well as the anticipation and excitement of the days ahead and then we will celebrate with joy the baby's birth."

They provided for all of her pre and post-natal needs. A huge Mother's Day card was sent to the mother by the parish which prayed for her throughout the pregnancy although they didn't even know her name. A baby shower was held and the parishioners brought hundreds of wrapped gifts to the weekend Masses. The baby was born and was baptized.

In January 1993, I returned to Chicago and met the mother and her new son, Michael, at a prayer meeting. She said that she wants to spend the rest of her life helping mothers and their unborn children. She said, "It's made all the difference in the world to know that there are people who are ready to help, people who care."

After the prayer meeting, the Image was brought to her home and baby Michael was brought to the Image and his hand was placed over Our Lady's heart. He left it there for a long time as if thankful that she had mediated the grace for his birth.

Our Lady also mediates the grace of forgiveness and reconciliation to those mothers who have been victims of abortion. Day after day, teenage girls and women fall victim to the evils of abortions and millions of innocent, precious babies fall victim to society's toleration of the holocaust.

One mother victim of abortion became pregnant in college. She was confused, hurt, misinformed and went to an abortuary for help. After being shuffled through some paperwork, tests and a "counselor" she was told that "it will be okay." She was not counseled on the option of giving birth and adoption.

"It was not okay," she reported. "I felt a ripping torment, hurt and devastation beyond description for killing my baby. Days turned into months which turned into years and I continued to carry the burden of shame, grief and guilt for ten long years. Then I attended a Marian Conference where a special blessing awaited me from Our Lady of Guadalupe through her Missionary Image. I went before her to pray and the next day I interviewed Dan Lynch."

This mother victim of abortion asked me, "How will Mary end abortion?" I replied that "she will melt hearts and the melted heart of a mother would never consider killing her innocent helpless child, she will reverence the life within her and bring it forth." At this point she broke down crying and told me, "I had an abortion ten years ago. You are the first person in the whole world that I have told. I named my son Joshua and have asked him to forgive me." I quickly arranged for her to receive the sacraments of Reconciliation and Eucharist that day for the first time since her abortion. We both felt great joy for her response to Our Lady's call to come back to the Sacred Heart of her Son and His holy Church.

Solar phenomenon which occurred at noon on June 9, 1991, over Mexico City when the first Missionary Image left for Central America. This was witnessed by millions. *(Reuters/Bettmann Newsphotos)*.

Missionary Image photograph in which an apparent Host appeared above Our Lady's fingertips.

Missionary **Image photograph in which an apparent Host appeared to the** right of her head in the **exact center of Our Lady's image.**

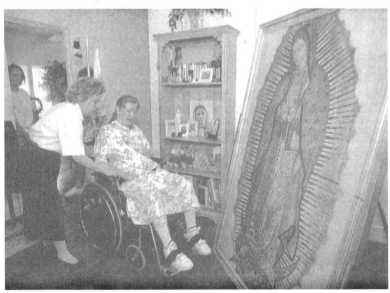

Missionary Image overlooking a young lady who was disabled in a car accident caused by a drunken driver. Her mother assists her and prays for the grace of quiet endurance and acceptance of her daughter's condition.

Missionary Image Cries Tears of Oil! The Missionary Image cried tears of oil on Christmas 1995 in Our Lady of Grace Church, Colchester, Vermont. The pastor, Father Brian Mead, preached that Our Lady was crying on her Son's birthday for those of her children who have no birthday because of abortion.

Our Lady's Tears

The Holy Father said, "Mary's tears are seen in her apparitions, with which, from time to time, she accompanies the Church during her journey on the highways of the world.

"Our Lady's tears belong to the order of signs: They testify to the presence of the mother in the Church and in the world. A mother weeps when she sees her children threatened by evil, be it spiritual or physical.

"These are the tears of sorrow for all those who refuse the love of God, for those families who are broken or in difficulty, for the young people seduced by a consumerist civilization and so often disoriented, for the violence that still spills so much blood and for the misunderstandings and hate which dig deep trenches between individuals and peoples.

"They are tears of prayer: The mother's prayer that gives strength to every other prayer, and that rises in supplication for all those who do not pray because they are distracted by a thousand other interests, or because they are obstinately closed to God's call.

"They are tears of hope, which melt the hardness of hearts and open them to meeting Christ the Redeemer, source of light and peace for individuals, for families, for the whole of society.

"O Lady of Tears, look with motherly goodness on the sorrow of the world! Dry the tears of the suffering, of the forgotten, of the desperate and of the victims of every violence.

"Make everyone weep tears of repentance and of new life, which will open their hearts to the regenerating gift of God's love. Make them weep tears of joy for having seen the profound tenderness of your heart. Praised be Jesus Christ!"

St. Louis' Great Flood Prematurely Recedes. I spoke at the St. Louis Eucharistic Congress during the height of the greatest flood in United States history. In my talk I explained how Our Lady of Guadalupe interceded to save Mexico City from a horrible flood in 1634. The flood had already killed 30,000 people. The desperate citizens, imploring Our Lady's help, carried the Miraculous Tilma through the knee-high flood waters from the Basilica to the Cathedral in Mexico City. This was the first and only time such a procession has taken place. The flood miraculously ended.

After my talk, I was asked by Congress attendees to take the Missionary Image to the flooding Mississippi River. This river was originally named the River of the Immaculate Conception. Our Lady of Gaudalupe is a representation of the Immaculate Conception.

I made an announcement that we were having a spontaneous procession with the Missionary Image to the river. About 200 people joined us as we processed from the Cathedral of St. Louis to the great arch of the Gateway to the West and down the flood-swept steps to the riverside. There we were joined by hundreds of on-lookers as we sprinkled holy water into the river and prayed in the pouring rain for an abatement of the flood, the salvation of the dead and the healing of the sufferers. We concluded by singing "America the Beautiful."

As we processed back, the rain suddenly stopped and as we sang the very last note of the "Hail Holy Queen", the cathedral bells unexpectedly rang out jubilantly at 5:20 pm! As we placed the Image into our van, a large flock of swallows suddenly swooped over and circled continously. There were no other birds seen anywhere else.

The next day the flood waters began to recede one day before the predicted high crest, which never came. The Congress organizers credited this to Our Lady of Guadalupe.

Missionary Image Visitations Bring Conversions and Save Lives!
After I gave a talk in Ottawa, Ontario, a woman approached me and asked me if any father of an aborted child had ever given witness of his sin. I replied that I had never heard from such a father in any of my travels throughout the world.

The very next person who spoke to me was a distressed-looking young man. Astonishingly, he said that he was one of the guilty fathers of an aborted child whom I had said were equally as responsible as the mothers, if not more so.

He said, "I killed two of my children for all of the common reasons that you mentioned - no money, no commitment, no responsibility. Then my favorite niece who was only an 18 month old baby was killed by her babysitter. I tossed all night asking, 'Why is this happening to me? Why am I in the middle of this murder?' Our Lady said to me, very clearly, 'Why do you ask, you did the same thing twice!'

"I was involved in the New Age and didn't know Our Lady. Shortly thereafter I was walking by a Catholic Church and saw a statue of Our Lady out in front if it. I fell to my knees in tears on the sidewalk before her. Soon I found myself entering Catholic churches and praying in the vestibules alone. Now I have entered the congregation and pray with everyone!"

One day, a pregnant mother named Helena waited inside an abortuary to have an abortion. Father Frank Pavone, National Director of Priests for Life, was praying with the Missionary Image and a group of pro-lifers outside. Helena looked outside, saw the Roman collar on Father Frank and thought, "There's a priest out there! What am I doing in here?!"

Helena changed her mind about the abortion, came outside and received the help of the pro-lifers. She later gave birth to her child, appropriately named *Guadalupe*, who was later baptized by Father Frank!

A pregnant mother named Cathy was told by her doctor that her placenta was damaged and she would probably have a

Father Frank Pavone, National Director of Priests for Life, with Helena and her daughter Guadalupe.

miscarriage. She called the Missionary Image apostolate and asked for prayers to Our Lady of Guadalupe. When Cathy returned to her doctor, a sonogram showed a healthy placenta! She later gave birth to a healthy son, Alexander.

Another repentant mother victim of abortion said, "I did not confess this horrid sin until after learning about Our Lady of Guadalupe. Her Image is beautiful, loving, and it draws me. Our Lady of Guadalupe guided me towards self-knowledge and the love and peace only possible through the sacrament of Penance."

A daughter lives because her pregnant mother decided against abortion when she arrived at the abortuary and saw the Missionary Image. Two years later when the Missionary Image returned to her area, the mother presented the child that she had almost killed to Our Lady of Guadalupe as the Protectress of the Unborn. She said, "My daughter's first word was 'Jesus' and I came to thank Our Lady of Guadalupe for saving her."

Our Lady of Guadalupe also saved another mother who had four abortions! She said, "I now consecrate myself daily to the holy Virgin Mother of Guadalupe and I ask her to make me an instrument to end abortion through melting hearts. I believe that Our Lady of Guadalupe will heal all those who have been wounded by the grave sin of abortion and that she is the shield that will protect the unborn children and their mothers."

In November 1992, four-year-old Alex Schuhmann lay dying in a Kentucky hospital of a rare lung disease, *bronchialitus obliterans*.

Guardian Debbie Womack, brought the Missionary Image to Alex's hospital room on the day doctors predicted she would die. Alex was lifted up to the Image and she tenderly touched and kissed Our Lady.

The next day, the doctors went to Alex's room and were shocked to find her playing and eating a hamburger! Alex's mother credits this saving healing to Our Lady of Guadalupe through her Missionary Image.

Alex Schuhmann smiles after her remarkable healing.

The saving of so many lives by Visitations of the Missionary Image should give us the courage to march on with confident hope!

PART FIVE

Our Lady of Guadalupe's Recent Requests

17. Repentance, Prayer and Fasting

As at Lourdes, Fatima and Medjugorje, Our Lady of Guadalupe's first recent requests are for repentance, prayer and fasting. She said, "I want all of the Americas to prepare for my visit to the United States of America by prayer, fasting, confession and repentance of sin . . . ." See Appendix A, First Message.

Repentance is a total interior change of heart which proceeds from an act of submission of our will to seek first the Kingdom of God. See Mt 3:2; 6:33.

Repentance consists of a radical reformation of our lives consisting of acknowledgment and confession of our sins; turning from the values of the world to those of Jesus Christ and faith and acceptance of His message and of His Person as the Son of God and our personal Lord and Savior causing through His grace an inner transformation producing fruits of prayer, self-denial and charity. See Acts 26:20. This is the foundation of all Christianity. See Heb 6:1-2.

Prayer and Fasting should proceed from an interior desire for union with God rather than be exhibited as external signs. Jesus condemned prayer said for the sake of notice. See Mt 6:5. He remarked upon the brief petition for pardon uttered

by the tax collector as the prayer that justifies a man. See
Lk 18:10 ff. Jesus also condemned the appearance of self-denial.
See Mt 6:16-18.

External fasting without interior love of God and neighbor
are really works for one's self. True fasting that delights the
Lord involves more of charity than self-denial. See Is 58:6-7;
Mt 9:13.

In our prayer we should recognize the un-redeemed sin within
us, offer it to Jesus for his redemption and continually yearn
to be closer to God. Our Lady said at Medjugorje, "You all
must understand that you have to pray. Prayer is not a trifle.
Prayer is a dialogue with God. You must hear the voice of
God in every prayer. It is not possible to live without prayer.
Prayer is life."

Our Lady also requests the daily Rosary, frequent
participation in the Holy Sacrifice of the Mass, Eucharistic
reception and adoration, and prayerful study of Scripture and
the teachings of the Church and obedience to them. See
Appendix A, First Message.

18. Join Under My Banner

Our Lady of Guadalupe said that "I want you to, immediately, place your entire pro-life force and efforts under my banner as Your Lady of Guadalupe. I will give you my powerful protection and help. I will lead you to victory over the forces of death which are preying upon babies in the wombs of their mothers." See Appendix A, First Message.

One practical way to respond to her request is to lead processions to abortion killing centers with an Image of Our Lady of Guadalupe. We should counsel the mothers, pray for exorcism of the demons present there and consecrate the victims of abortion (staff, mothers and children) to the Sorrowful and Immaculate Heart of Mary, Our Lady of Guadalupe, Protectress of the Unborn. The Rosary should also be prayed there and Marian hymns sung. See Appendices G and H for Exorcism and Abortion Victim Prayers.

This should all be done in an atmosphere of a lawful, peaceful, prayerful presence at the killing center, preferably preceded by a Mass. Those unable to be present at the killing center should go before the Blessed Sacrament in prayer support.

We should form this prayerful presence in imitation of Our Lady who stood in prayer at the feet of her innocent crucified Son. Our presence at the killing center is the last barrier between the unborn child's life and death. It is the mother's last hope. It is good for us to be there!

Our Lady of Guadalupe claimed Tepeyac Hill for herself from Tonantzin, the false mother goddess. A hill that was used for idols was converted to one that was used to revere life through the intercession of the Mother of the Americas. She said, "Here I will demonstrate . . . all my love . . . and my protection to the people." In the same way, she can convert killing centers to places where life is revered and demonstrate her love and protection there.

Our Lady of Guadalupe has requested that all pro-life forces be placed under her banner because her image has such supernatural significance and power. This is the only true image of Our Lady on earth and it reflects her mission and power given to her from the beginning to crush the head of Satan. See Gn 3:15 and Rev 12. As such, it has great power over Satan and his demons.

This image of Our Lady of Guadalupe was the Great Sign which was presented to Satan in all of the grandeur in which it had been conceived in the divine mind. See Rev 12. This Great Sign revealed the divine plan to create and redeem mankind through God incarnate in a "Woman," Our Lady of Guadalupe.

Satan and the bad angels rebelled against this divine plan. The good and obedient angels were led by St. Michael in a spiritual battle against them. St. Michael used the Great Sign as a shield and arm of battle and cast Satan and the bad angels into hell. See Rev 12:7-8.

This is why the image of Our Lady of Guadalupe, with St. Michael below her leading her forward, is so effective in our spiritual warfare today. It is through this image that Our Lady of Guadalupe promises that she "will lead you to victory over the forces of death which are preying upon babies in the wombs of their mothers."

A variety of images and a Supernatural Rescue Mission booklet containing prayers, psalms and hymns for a prayerful presence to end abortion may be ordered through the Publisher.

Missionary Image in front of Toronto, Ontario abortion killing center with signs of the fruits of the Holy Spirit.

St. Michael the Archangel carrying banner of Our Lady of Guadalupe and defeating Satan. See Rev 12:7-8.

19. Total Consecration

Our Lady of Guadalupe said that "as you go forth under my banner as Your Lady of Guadalupe, you will have no better guide than what my faithful son, St. Louis de Montfort, recommends as the True Devotion to me." See Appendix A, First Message.

True Devotion is a book written by St. Louis Marie Grignion de Montfort in which he teaches the Total Consecration to Jesus through Mary. St. Louis was a priest born in Montfort-La-Canne, France on January 31, 1673. He dropped his full name and became known simply as St. Louis de Montfort, after his home town.

He was a simple but wise priest who was much opposed, misunderstood and maligned as he preached missions from diocese to diocese. He once walked 1000 miles all the way to Rome and back to receive confirmation from Pope Clement XI that he was following God's will. The Pope appointed him as a Missionary Apostolic for all of France yet he was still banned from six dioceses!

Father Faber said that St. Louis "comes forward like another St. Vincent Ferrer, as if on the days bordering on the Last Judgment, and proclaims that he brings an authentic message from God about the greater honor and wider knowledge and more prominent love of His Blessed Mother, and her connection with the second advent of her Son."

St. Louis prophesied concerning his own book that, ". . . raging beasts shall come in fury to tear with their diabolical teeth this little writing and him whom the Holy Ghost has made use of to write it - or at least to smother it in the darkness and silence of a coffer, that it may not appear. They shall even attack and persecute those who shall read it and carry it out in practice." This prophecy was literally fulfilled and the manuscript for the book was not found until 1842 in a chest of old books.

St. Louis died, exhausted from his many labors, at the age of 43 on April 28, 1716. He was canonized as a saint in 1947. He is truly a saint for our times.

St. Louis also prophesied that God with His holy Mother would form great souls as apostles of the latter times. He said, "these great souls, full of grace and zeal, shall be chosen to match themselves against the enemies of God, who shall rage on all sides; and they shall be singularly devout to our Blessed Lady, illuminated by her light, strengthened with her nourishment, led by her spirit, supported by her arm and sheltered under her protection, so that they shall fight with one hand and build with the other . . . . They will know the grandeurs of that Queen, and will consecrate themselves entirely to her service as subjects and slaves of love . . . . They shall be the true apostles of the latter times . . . ."

In June of 1992, a historic meeting occurred in Washington, D.C. This was a meeting of the United States Catholic Apostolate Leaders representing 76 different apostolates. The number one priority established by this meeting was the practice of St. Louis' True Devotion by a daily consecration to Jesus through Mary. This meeting concluded with a consecration of these apostolates to Our Lady of Guadalupe and a prayer that all apostolates would unite in spirit under her banner as the Queen and Mother of the Americas.

In his encyclical, *Mother of the Redeemer*, Pope John Paul II cites St. Louis' book and of *all* the many teachers of Marian spirituality he recalls *only* the figure of St. Louis and states that "there thus exists solid points of reference to look to and follow in the context of this Marian Year." The Pope's principal point of reference is to St. Louis' *True Devotion* in which he teaches Total Consecration to Jesus through Mary as a means of renewing our Baptismal promises.

This is the consecration personally made and lived by Pope John Paul II and recommended by him to us. As such, we should imitate him, follow his recommendation and make St. Louis' Total Consecration.

By this Total Consecration we renounce Satan, his pomps and works and voluntarily offer, in love without reserve, to Jesus through Our Lady all that we have in the order of nature and in the order of grace. We offer our entire selves, body and soul, and all that we possess and even the merits of our prayers and good works past, present and for all eternity to be disposed of wholly according to His will. St. Louis' Act of Total Consecration is contained in Appendix C.

This Act of Consecration is distinguished from any other consecration formula to Our Lady by its totality, its permanency and the gift of the merits of our prayers and good works. Consequently, it is the most perfect consecration formula and most perfectly fulfills Our Lady's requests to consecrate ourselves to her Immaculate Heart.

By the Total Consecration we become possessed by Our Lady, belong to her from moment to moment and become transformed by her into the image of her Son Jesus. She takes our Total Consecration at our word so that at each moment we will be dependent upon her and she will act in us and with us. We will tenderly and gently think, speak, act, pray and love as does Our Lady. We live this consecration by expecting her leading in our lives and her providing for all of our needs at every moment. Therefore, we walk in docile simplicity and total abandonment.

Total Consecration to Our Lady means that we entrust ourselves to her and accept her mediation of our self-offering to Jesus, the source of our redemption. It does not consist in transitory affection or emotion but proceeds from true faith, hope and love.

St. Louis tells us that the Total Consecration is made to Jesus through Mary, and is a perfect renewal of our Baptismal vows by which we voluntarily renounce Satan, his pomps and his works, and take Jesus for our Lord as a slave of love.

This slavery is the same slavery as spoken of by Saint Paul. See Rom 1:1; Gal 1:10; Phil 1:1 and Tit 1:1. It is a slavery of the will according to the examples of Jesus (see Phil 2:7) and Our Lady. See Lk 1:38. It is the obedience of faith. Since Jesus and Our Lady have the same will and have us as the same slaves, we are then the loving slaves of Our Lady so that we will be more perfect slaves of Jesus.

Pope John Paul II has made and lives St. Louis' Total Consecration. He has taken from St. Louis as his papal motto "totus tuus" meaning totally yours. He has endorsed St. Louis' Total Consecration as the best means of participating fruitfully and effectively in the mystery of the redemption.

When he was a young man clandestinely studying for the priesthood during the Nazi occupation, St. Louis' treatise on *True Devotion* providentially came into his hands. He initially met two obstacles in studying it. He was afraid that devotion to Our Lady would detract from the precedence of Christ and he was impeded by the baroque style of the book's language. He soon overcame both of these obstacles and so should we.

He found that our inner relation to the Mother of God derives from our connection with the mystery of Christ. Therefore, there is no question of the one preventing us from seeing the other.

In spite of the book's baroque style the Pope found that it dealt with something fundamental and it was not enough merely to have read it once. He remembers carrying it on himself for a long time even to the sodium factory where he worked which resulted in spotting it with lime. Even he had to re-read it to understand it. He continually went back to certain passages and declares that the reading of the book was a decisive turning point in his life.

He said, " 'Perfect devotion to Mary' - that is how the author of the treatise puts it - that is, the true knowledge of her, and confident surrender to her, grows with our knowledge of Christ and our confident surrender to His person. What is more, this 'perfect devotion' is indispensable to anyone who means to give himself without reserve to Christ and to the work of redemption. Grignion de Montfort even shows us the working of the mysteries which quicken our faith and make it grow and render it fruitful. The more my inner life has been centered on the mystery of the redemption, the more surrender to Mary, in the spirit of St. Louis Grignion de Montfort, has seemed to me the best means of participating fruitfully and effectively in this reality, in order to draw from it and share with others its inexpressible riches."

On August 15, 1992, the Feast of the Assumption of the Blessed Virgin Mary, Father Walter Winrich and myself led over 1,000 faithful in making the Total Consecration of St. Louis de Montfort at the base of the mountain of the Mother Cabrini Shrine in Golden, Colorado. Then we all processed with the Missionary Image and the visionary, Veronica Garcia, up the stairway past the Stations of the Cross to the summit where we recited the Glorious Mysteries of the Rosary.

Veronica saw large angels lined up on both sides of the stairway all the way to the top of the mountain where angels were located everywhere. The Missionary Image, Veronica and myself went to the bush where Our Lady appears and I began to lead the Rosary. As I ended the first decade, Veronica, who was crushed against me by the faithful, went into ecstacy. She shook, cried and lifted her arms to the sky. She later described her vision:

"The sky in front of me opened up, almost like a curtain being drawn open, and in the center appeared two hearts - the Sacred Heart of Jesus and the Immaculate Heart of Mary. On either side were thousands of angels singing their praises. (I have never heard the songs before and I doubt that I will ever hear anything like it on earth). The two hearts came together and fused into one heart. Then Our Lady appeared with this one heart pulsating out of the center of her chest with thousands of rays radiating everywhere. She was dressed in an ivory dress with a beautiful blue mantle. On her head was a wreath of red roses and stars all around.

"The angels came to each person and took each heart to present to our Mother who, in turn, presented each heart to Jesus, who in turn, fused each heart into His own Sacred Heart. The angels were then given a blood-red rosebud by Our Lady to place back where the heart of each person had been.

"This rosebud was planted in order to bloom into an actual Tree of Life. Then I witnessed an immediate 'branding' on the forehead of each person with the Sign of the Cross in the flame of the Holy Spirit. Then, for the second time ever, Our Lady allowed me to witness her as she prayed the Magnificat to God the Father (whom I did not see). Our Lady gave me the understanding that I was to later open the book *God Alone*, which contains the collected writings of St. Louis de Montfort, and she would open it to the explanation of what we were to do with the rosebud that was given to us. Then Our Lady said:

'My children: You are now enrolled in the Army of Christ. You belong to us my angels. You are the delight of the heavens on this day. A special place has been prepared for you for all eternity. I love you and I am with you always.' "

Our Lady told Veronica that by our Total Consecration we were "enrolled in the Army of Christ." Similarly, Our Lady told Father Gobbi on November 1, 1973, the Feast of All Saints, that those consecrated to her Immaculate Heart should form her "Great White Army." She said, "Through them my light will once again shine in the midst of the great darkness, and my immaculate whiteness in the midst of so much corruption of death."

Later, during her talk on the evening of her apparition, Our Lady led Veronica to open the book *God Alone* in order to explain the planting by the angels of the rosebud in our hearts. Veronica opened the book to where St. Louis teaches that the true Tree of Life that the Holy Spirit plants in a soul is the Total Consecration. This Tree or Total Consecration should be carefully cultivated by us so that it will yield its fruit, Jesus Christ in us, in due season.

St. Louis teaches that this Tree of Life once planted in a docile heart must be cultivated by fresh air, that is by Our Lady only and not by human support or our own efforts. Like a good gardener we must protect this Tree against harm. Thorns and thistles which choke the Tree, such as pleasures of the flesh, must be cut away and rooted out by self-denial, fasting and mortification of the senses. Grubs which eat the leaves of the Tree, such as self-love, must be removed. Destructive animals which eat the Tree, such as sins, must not be allowed near it. The Tree must also be watered by reception of the sacraments and prayers.

So long as we care for this Tree we need not fear the strong winds of temptation or its destruction by the elements. The Tree will yield its fruit in due season. The fruit is Jesus Christ, in whom we will be transformed by Our Lady whose only fruit is her son Jesus.

Prayer cenacles are a great help for us to make, live and share with others this Total Consecration. Pope John Paul II in his encyclical on the Holy Spirit said, "I see all the Church in a cenacle." Cenacles are groups who pray for the coming of the Holy Spirit through Total Consecration to the Immaculate Heart of Mary in the spirit of St. Louis de Montfort.

For years Our Lady has been insistently asking us to "multiply cenacles." By their very nature, they are settings for growth in personal holiness. They result in apostolic activity in union with Our Lady.

After the Ascension of Jesus into heaven, Our Lady and the Apostles gathered in the Upper Room of the Last Supper in Jerusalem where they devoted themselves to constant prayer (see Acts 1:13-14) and awaited and received the Holy Spirit on Pentecost. Immediately thereafter they began their apostolic activity. This was the first "cenacle." This term was derived from the Latin *cena* meaning "supper" with reference to the room of the Last Supper and Pentecost.

Today Our Lady calls us to come together in cenacles to unite with her to pray, to fraternally share and to expectantly await and receive the Holy Spirit in the prodigy of the New Pentecost. From cenacles come Spirit-empowered apostolic activity. Prayer cenacles need no complex organization. Discussions about goals, plans, objectives and feverish activity would be out of place. Everything should be simple, spontaneous, quiet, fraternal and familial.

Cenacles of the Immaculate Heart of Mary may be composed of as few as two or three persons. As a general norm there should be a maximum of twelve. They may consist of families, priests, religious, faithful or mixed. Such cenacles may take place whenever and wherever two or three or more come together with Our Lady to pray and to share.

The objects of Cenacles of the Immaculate Heart of Mary are to prepare, make and renew our Total Consecration to the Immaculate Heart of Mary and to live our consecration. We do this by growing in union with the Sacred Heart through the Immaculate Heart of Mary and through apostolic activity to evangelize our environment (particularly through distributing images of Our Lady of Guadalupe) in order to convert others and to end abortion.

The suggested format of such a cenacle is a one to two hour weekly gathering in the presence of an image of Our Lady of Guadalupe to do the following:

1. Invoke the Holy Spirit and pray for the Pope.
2. Recite a Rosary of at least five decades.
3. Read from *True Devotion* by St. Louis de Montfort and *To The Priests*, messages of Our Lady to Father Stefano Gobbi. The first work explains St. Louis' teaching on Total Consecration and the second work explains how to live a life of consecration on a daily basis. These works are contained in a Cenacle Formation Packet available from the Publisher.
4. Share reflections on these readings.

5. Share insights and experiences in living a life of consecration to the Immaculate Heart of Mary.
6. Share reports on apostolic activities of the prior week.
7. Renew our consecration to the Immaculate Heart of Mary.
8. Close with prayer of thanksgiving and Sign of the Cross in blessing.

Cenacle members should use St. Louis' *Preparation for Total Consecration* to make or renew this consecration as soon as possible, considering the members' capabilities and the guidance of Our Lady and the Holy Spirit. Cenacles of the Immaculate Heart of Mary are ideal for learning, making and then living this consecration. The consecration can be made in a Cenacle Consecration Ceremony which is explained in the Consecration Formation Packet available from the Publisher.

This consecration is not an act that is made once and then forgotten. It is a way of life totally at Our Lady's disposal. By it we do all our actions *by* Mary, *with* Mary, *in* Mary and *for* Mary.

As we live this consecration, our lives become truly transformed. Our Lady helps us to become more abandoned, docile, simple and humble, confidently trusting always and only in God. She is then able to act through us, as we allow her and submit ourselves to her maternal action. In this manner, we imitate Jesus in His complete obedience to and reliance on His Mother.

Our Lady will form us through our consecration into the likeness of her Son. Then we will have the strength to march forth under her banner as she says, "with no better guide than . . . the True Devotion to me." See Appendix A, First Message.

Cenacles will empower us to engage in apostolic activities to end abortion and bring conversions as the Apostles brought conversions after the Pentecost experience in their cenacle with Our Lady. See Acts 2:41.

Local circumstances, creativity and inspiration will suggest many forms of apostolic activity for members of cenacles.

Among the various possibilities are a lawful, peaceful, prayerful, presence at abortion killing centers on a regular basis; sidewalk counselling and the establishment of crisis pregnancy centers near killing centers as an alternative for mothers who seek abortion; burying of aborted children; praying for the salvation of their souls, erecting monuments to remember them and having Masses said for them and to end abortion.

Some apostolic activities to bring others to conversion would be to multiply cenacles of the Immaculate Heart of Mary; multiply images by telling the story of Our Lady of Guadalupe and distributing her images; multiply Rosaries among parish groups, at killing centers, etc.; multiply consecrations to the Immaculate Heart of Mary; and to multiply conversions by being a personal witness for Christ in your environment.

All of these will be by, with, in and for the Immaculate Heart of Mary and all to the greater glory of God!

Visionary Veronica Garcia in ecstacy next to the Missionary Image and author at Mother Cabrini Shrine, Golden, Colorado. Her vision is explained in Chapter 19.

20. Prayer for the Marian Movement of Priests

Our Lady of Guadalupe requests that we "pray for and support my beloved priests in the Marian Movement of Priests." See Appendix A, First Message.

The Marian Movement of Priests is a spiritual movement of priests and laity who promulgate the messages of Our Lady as contained in the book, *To the Priests, Our Lady's Beloved Sons.*

Our Lady's messages are given to Father Stefano Gobbi, a simple Italian priest. On May 8, 1972, he was praying at Fatima for some priests who were in rebellion against the Church's authority. He was inspired to have confidence in the Immaculate Heart of Mary who would use him as a humble instrument to gather faithful priests to defend the Pope.

Our Lady later told him, "I have chosen you because you are the least apt instrument; thus no one will say that this is your work. The Marian Movement of Priests must be my work alone. Through your weakness, I will manifest my strength; through your nothingness, I will manifest my power."

Our Lady's messages are in the form of a conversation between a mother and her child. As with a mother, some themes are insistently repeated. Eventually these messages were compiled in the book, *To The Priests, Our Lady's Beloved Sons.*

Like Our Lady of Guadalupe's recent requests, these messages call for a renewed spirit of prayer and penance; fervent participation in the celebration of the Eucharist and in the apostolate; the daily recitation of the Rosary; an austere manner of life; practice of the Christian virtues, especially purity and union with and prayer for the Pope and the bishops and priests in union with him.

Prayers for priests is an ardent wish of Our Lady of Guadalupe. We should not criticize priests and Bishops but should pray for their sanctification so that we will have them as guardians of the faith.

More information on the Total Consecration and the Marian Movement of Priests is contained in the author's book, *The Call to Total Consecration to the Immaculate Heart of Mary,* available from the Publisher.

21. Devotion to the Holy Angels

Our Lady of Guadalupe said, "I will send my angels to your side during all of your battles against the evil one and his works." See Appendix A, First Message.

Angels are pure spirits. In the beginning of time, God created heaven and earth and angels as pure spirits. See Col 1:16. They were created as immortal beings out of the goodness of God for His glorification. See Heb 2:10. They were endowed with grace but were subjected to a moral testing. They were given a one-time fundamental option to acknowledge God as their maker and Lord and to serve Him or not.

The good angels who passed the test were rewarded with the blessedness of heaven. See Mt 18:10. Satan (meaning Adversary) and the bad angels who did not pass the test through their own sin fell from heaven and were eternally damned (see 2 Pet 2:4; Jude 6) even though they knew that such would be the consequence of their disobedience!

Satan, the evil one, was indulged in self-love through his awareness that he had greater gifts of nature and grace than all of the other angels. He failed to give gratitude for those gifts to God who was the source of them all.

God revealed to the angels that he would create a human nature lower than themselves which the Son would incarnate as true God and true man and that they must adore and obey Him. God also revealed to them that the Son would be born of a "Woman" who would be Queen of all creatures and that they would have to acknowledge her as a superior conjointly with the Son. The good angels submitted themselves to these commands.

In his pride, however, Satan aspired to be the head of all angels and men, demanded that the Incarnation be consummated in him and refused to acknowledge his inferiority to the "Woman." This mysterious "Woman" is the Woman of Genesis (see Gn 3:15) and the Woman of Revelation. See Rev 12. She is Our Lady of Guadalupe.

Satan induced many angel followers to disobey the divine commands and pursuaded them that he would be their chief and that he would set up a government independent and separate from Christ. He vowed to persecute and destroy human nature, the Woman and Jesus. Satan's challenge was, "I will not serve, I will not acknowledge God!"

The good and obedient angels were led by Michael in a spiritual battle of intellects and wills against Satan and the bad angels. Using the Great Sign of the Woman Clothed with the Sun (see Rev 12:1), Our Lady of Guadalupe, as a shield and arm of battle, Michael, the prince of the heavenly hosts, by the divine power of God cast into hell Satan and the bad angels with his invincible battle cry, "Who is like unto God?"

This battle is told in a mystical sense by St. John in the twelfth chapter of the Book of Revelation which can be understood in the past tense as applying to the fall of the bad angels and in the future tense as applying to the ultimate condemnation of them and their followers by the triumph of the Immaculate Heart of Mary and the reign of Christ.

We should pray the battle prayer of St. Michael the Archangel, composed by Pope Leo XIII in the late nineteenth century when he saw in a vision the satanic evil to come in this twentieth century. The angels protect us and help us towards our salvation. We should also pray to our guardian angels.

Our guardian angels are very real and very powerful. God wants us to have a good relationship with them and to cooperate with them on our path to eternal life.

This relationship begins with our obedience to our guardian angels when they speak to us in the voice of our conscience. To do this we must become more interiorly silent so that we can hear this voice and obey it. Gradually, we will hear this voice more clearly, discern it as God's will and promptly follow it.

With practice and humble docility, we will soon build a good working relationship with our guardian angels. We should ask God to give us through our guardian angels more light, more protection, more rule and more guidance. Our guardian angels will soon bring us to love their greatest function which is to adore God present in the Blessed Sacrament. With them we will adore and pray, "holy, holy, holy, Lord God of Hosts . . . ."

St. Michael
Power of God

St. Raphael
Doctor of God

THE FOUR ANGELS OF TEPEYAC HILL

St. Gabriel
Messenger of God

St. Uriel
Sentry of God

22. Devotion to St. Joseph

Our Lady of Guadalupe said, "did not Joseph, in obedience to a message of an angel from God, protect my Baby, the Infant Jesus, and me from harm? Did he not protect us on our journey to and from Egypt? Holy Joseph will do the same for my journey throughout the Americas when you call upon him. With the help of my Joseph and your own prudent care, my Image will make the entire journey safely." See Appendix A, Third Message.

Our Lady recalls to us the Flight to Egypt (see Mt 2:13-15) and sets Joseph up as an example for us to be followed in promptly obeying our angels. We remember that "Joseph got up and took the Child and His Mother and left *that night* for Egypt." Mt 2:14. Our Lady does not wish us to use merely human wisdom and to act for human respect. She said: "You, my children, do not serve me and my request to travel throughout the width and breath of the Americas by using worldly wisdom, logic, caution and a concern for human respect. As obedient children, you will serve me by immediate actions based on complete trust in my motherly love and concern for you. You do your part and I will do mine." See Appendix A, Second Message.

St. Joseph is the supreme example of such obedience and complete trust in God. We should venerate him, follow his good example and pray to him as the Protector of the Unborn and the Family as we meditate on his protection of Our Lady and the unborn Christ Child as they journeyed to Bethlehem. See Lk 2:4. St. Joseph is the patron saint of the Missionary Image apostolate.

St. Joseph, Protector of Family Life, shown on banner with Our Lady of Guadalupe and Unborn Irish Child, Mullingar, Ireland.

23. Provide Replicas of My Image

Our Lady of Guadalupe requested: "Provide a replica of my Image to the Bishops of each country, territory and island of the Americas. As the replicas travel their paths out from my Image, those paths become rays of my love, care, protection and help for all my children everywhere." See Appendix A, Fifth Message.

In response to this request, the apostolate of the Missionary Image helped to obtain replica images from the Basilica in Mexico City for these different geographic areas.

These replicas were brought to Santo Domingo in the Dominican Republic where Columbus first landed. There Pope John Paul II celebrated a Mass on October 12, 1992, to celebrate the 500th anniversary of the evangelization of the Americas. Most of the Bishops of the Americas attended the Mass, the Pope blessed the replica images and they were distributed to the Bishops of the Americas. One of these Images was sent to the apostolate of the Missionary Image and was provided by it for Canada. Our Lady's request has been answered.

These replicas will help to realize Our Lady's hopes that "all in the Americas may see me with their own eyes and know deeply the great love I have for each one of you, my children. . . . Give me the attention that you have always wanted to give me, the Ever Virgin, the Mother of the True God. You, my children of the Americas, have a very special place in my plans for bringing all to the Sacred Heart of my Son Jesus through my Immaculate Heart. In my plan, the journey of my Image throughout all of the Americas, is necessary." See Appendix A, Fourth Message.

"Please return to me, your Lady of Guadalupe, with your whole heart and the gift of your hands for my work." See Appendix A, Sixth Message.

PART SIX

The Victorious
Queen of Peace

24. Warnings, Chastisements and
Spiritual Warfare

"Hear, you leaders of Jacob, rulers of the House of Israel! Is it not your duty to know what is right, you who hate what is good, and love evil? You who tear their skin from them, and their flesh from their bones! They eat the flesh of my people, and flay their skin from them, and break their bones." Mi 3:1-3.

Such is the consequence of the sin of abortion which tears and flays the skin and the flesh of the unborn which is "eaten" through transplants of their fetal tissue into other humans.

Like the leaders of Jacob, this was "legalized" by *our* leaders through President Clinton on January 22, 1993, the 20th anniversary of the United States Supreme Court's "legalization" of abortion. On this one day he eliminated all of the prior presidential pro-life gains, particularly the ban on fetal transplants. All who knowingly voted for him will be held accountable for these abominations.

Sixty-four percent of all Catholics voted for Mr. Clinton or Ross Perot, both of whom clearly stated that they were "pro-choice" for abortion. Never was the choice between life and death so clearly presented to Catholics as a test of their faith.

Never have they so miserably failed the test. Catholics never had a vote when the United States Supreme Court "legalized" abortion. The election of 1992 gave the Catholics a clear choice to vote for a president who supported life or for a candidate who supported death.

Moses said, "I call heaven and earth today to witness against you; I have set before you life and death, the blessing and the curse. Choose life, then, that you and your descendants may live . . . ." Deut 30:19. But Americans chose death and the curse. "Therefore, thus says the Lord God; See I am coming at you! I will inflict punishments in your midst while the nations look on. Because of all your abominations, I will do with you what I have never done before, the like of which I will never do again." Ez 5:8-9.

God never inflicts chastisements without warning us through His servants, the prophets. God's love for His sinful children is shown through the prophets who issue warnings to turn back to God and pray and fast for peace or suffer chastisements. Jonah warned Nineveh of its destruction but the people repented, prayed, fasted, and lived in peace. On the contrary, Jesus warned Jerusalem of its destruction but the people did not listen and Jerusalem was annihilated. Jesus prophesied that not a stone upon a stone would be left in Jerusalem because they did not recognize the path to peace. See Lk 19:41-44. This prophecy was literally fulfilled in the year 70 A.D. by the Roman General Titus who destroyed the city.

Cortes warned the Aztecs that if they did not cease human sacrifice he would annihilate Mexico City. They didn't listen to him and he annihilated the city in a 93 day siege, just as the Roman General Titus annihilated Jerusalem, leaving not a stone upon a stone standing.

In these times, God has sent us as His prophets His Mother and the Holy Father, Pope John Paul II. Our Lady appeared at Fatima, Portugal in 1917 and warned us to turn to God or to face annihilation but that in the end her Immaculate Heart would triumph and there would be an era of peace. Our Lady now appears throughout the world pleading for prayer and fasting to end abortion and bring conversions and peace or to suffer chastisements.

She warned Father Gobbi of the Marian Movement of Priests, "Abortions - these killings of innocent children, that cry for vengeance before the face of God - have spread and are performed in every part of this country. The moment of the divine justice and mercy has arrived! You will know the hour of weakness and poverty; the hour of suffering and defeat; the purifying hour of the great chastisements."

In 1973, at Akita, Japan, Our Lady said, "If men do not repent and better themselves, the Father will inflict a terrible punishment on all humanity. It will be a punishment greater than the deluge, such as one will never have seen before. Fire will fall from the sky and will wipe out a great part of humanity . . . ."

Similarly, St. Peter said that the godless "deliberately ignore the fact that the heavens existed of old and earth was formed out of water and through water by the word of God; through these the world that then existed was destroyed, deluged with water. The present heavens and earth have been reserved by the same word for fire, kept for the day of judgment and of destruction of the godless." 2 Pt 3:5-7.

In 1976, the Holy Father (as Cardinal Wojtyla) warned us that "We are standing in the face of the greatest historical confrontation humanity has gone through . . . . We are now facing the FINAL CONFRONTATION between the Church and the anti-Church, of the gospel versus the anti-gospel."

In 1979, the Holy Father stood in front of the United States Supreme Court justices who had "legalized" abortion and said, "When the sacredness of life before birth is attacked, we will STAND UP and proclaim that no one ever has the authority to destroy unborn life." However, we left the Holy Father standing alone and we did not stand up with him. Since then, we have allowed fifteen million innocent, helpless, American unborn babies to be killed by abortion.

So, in 1987, the Holy Father issued his last warning to America. "The CONDITION for the SURVIVAL of AMERICA is to respect every human person, especially the weakest and most defenseless ones, those as yet unborn."

This is the severest prophetic warning that this country has ever received. It tells us that the very condition for our nation's survival is to end abortion.

But the righteous and devout shall be preserved. "For if God did not spare the angels when they sinned, but condemned them to the chains of Tartarus and handed them over to be kept for judgment; and if He did not spare the ancient world, even though He preserved Noah, a herald of righteousness, together with seven others, when He brought a flood upon the godless world; and if He condemned the cities of Sodom and Gomorrah to destruction, reducing them to ashes, making them an example for the godless people of what is coming; and if He rescued Lot, a righteous man oppressed by the licentious conduct of unprincipled people . . . then the Lord knows how to rescue the devout from trial and to keep the unrighteous under punishment for the day of judgment . . . ." 2 Pt 2:4-9.

If we look carefully at the bottom of the image of Our Lady of Guadalupe, we will see her right foot showing beneath her long dress. Closer inspection will show this foot to be a baby's face. The folds of Our Lady's dress look like a blanket surrounding the baby like a papoose. But the baby is upside down! This is because the whole moral order is upside down because of "legalized" abortion and "upside down" thinking.

Some legislators now say that abortion is not only a "right" but a "good." To this the prophet Isaiah says, "Woe to those who call evil good, and good evil . . . ." Is 5:20.

Another sign from Our Lady of Guadalupe regarding the horror of abortion was given to John Bird, the film producer. John received special permission to videotape the original tilma within three feet for his video production, *River of Light*. A photograph of the tilma shows a sword-like beam of light which proceeds down the right side of the image. This photograph is shown on the inside of the back cover of this book.

A mystic revealed that this is a sword which points to the upside down head of the innocent martyr, St. John the Baptist. See Mk 6:25. His head in the image represents the innocent unborn children killed by abortion. St. John's head is upside down because abortion is "upside down" and against the natural order. Our Lady weeps for these innocents. See Mt 2:18.

This sword which represents the instrument of the injustice of killing the innocent unborn also represents the instrument of the justice of God to whom their blood cries out for vengeance. "But this is the day of the Lord God of Hosts, a day of vengeance, vengeance on his foes! The sword devours, is sated, drunk with their blood: for the Lord God of Hosts holds a slaughter feast . . . ." Jer 46:10.

This "slaughter" will be a slaughter of our false idols of pride, materialism, selfishness and "choice" through which the modern world has practiced and condoned sterilization, artificial contraception and abortion. This is God's justice which awaits the supporters of these abominations.

"The sins of the House of Israel are great beyond measure; the land is filled with bloodshed, the city with lawlessness. They think that the Lord has forsaken the land, that he does not see them. I, however, will not look upon them with pity nor show any mercy. I will bring their conduct upon their heads." Ez 9:9-10.

So the conduct of the modern worshippers of the false idols will come back upon their own heads. God's Day will come when he will say "Enough!" And the false idols will come tumbling down through the intercession of Our Lady of Guadalupe just as they did in pagan Aztec Mexico. The idols of materialism, selfishness and "choice" will fall through economic depression and natural disasters. There will be no time or opportunity for idle pursuits of these false idols. Our time will be spent on the simplicities of the necessities of food, clothing and shelter, love of neighbor and love and worship of the one true God. So let us be prepared as the day of the Lord draws near.

"Therefore, brothers, since through the Blood of Jesus, we have confidence of entrance into the sanctuary by the new and living way He opened for us through the veil, that is, His flesh, and since we have 'a great priest over the house of God,' let us approach with a sincere heart and in absolute trust, with our hearts sprinkled clean from an evil conscience and our bodies washed in pure water. Let us hold unwaveringly to our confession that gives us hope, for He who made the promises trustworthy. We must consider how to arouse one another to love and good works. We should not stay away from our assembly, as is the custom of some, but encourage one another, and this all the more as you see the day growing near." Heb 10:19-25.

The heads of those who are consecrated to Our Lady are protected. These heads are marked with the Sign of the Cross on their foreheads and, like the Israelites whose door posts were marked with the blood of the lamb, the angel of death shall pass over us.

If we look at St. John's forehead on John Bird's photograph, we see a cross of light, the tau (or "x"), the Sign of the Cross which is the seal of divine protection. "Pass through the city and mark an 'x' on the foreheads of those who moan and groan over all the abominations that are practiced within it. To the others I heard him say: Pass through the city after him and strike! Do not look on them with pity or show any mercy! Old men, youths and maidens, women and children - wipe them out! But do not touch any marked with the 'x' . . . ." Ez 10:4-6.

This Cross was "branded" on the foreheads of those who made St. Louis' Total Consecration as witnessed by the visionary Veronica Garcia and described in Chapter 19. It is by this consecration that we receive this mark of divine protection.

Abortion is a horrible evil because it is a direct attack against God, the Author of human life. It is a re-crucifixion of the innocent helpless Christ who said, "Whatever you do to the least of my brothers, that you do to me." Mt 25:45.

Abortion is a direct attack by Satan against innocents and against motherhood. Therefore, it is a direct attack against Jesus and His Holy Mother, Mary.

Abortion killing centers are the Calvaries of the modern world. Because it is there that Jesus is continually re-crucified and put to death in the millions of innocent babies killed. At these Calvaries, Jesus repeats again the moments of his crucifixion. There, with Him, is His Sorrowful Mother. She wants us to remain there with her, like the Apostle John, to keep watch with her in intercessory prayer, in faith, hope and in mercy and love for the mothers and their children who are killed there.

One woman who was praying in front of a killing center felt as if Our Lady said to her, " It is good for you to be here, as I stood at the foot of the Cross, silently watching and praying as my innocent Son was crucified." We should imitate Our Lady who stood at the foot of her Son's Cross prayerfully interceding for the killers and the victims.

Abortion and the evils of our times are beyond human redemption. Education, dialogue and political activity cannot save us from them. Only God can save us from them through Our Lady's intercession and our help through reparative prayer and fasting. Reparation helps to repair for the damage of sin. We should STAND UP as John did with Our Lady, in union with the Holy Father who said that we would do this when the sacredness of life before birth is attacked.

We must realize that Satan exists and that we are not involved in a merely natural battle against humans but also in a supernatural battle against Satan and the demons in spiritual warfare. St. Paul said, "Our battle is not against human forces but against . . . the rulers of this world of darkness, the evil spirits in regions above." Eph 6:12. Jesus said, "This kind does not leave but by prayer and fasting." Mt 17:21. We join Our Lady's army against them through the Total Consecration to her Immaculate Heart and use the spiritual weapons of reparative prayer, fasting and apostolic activity.

"The Dragon (Satan) became angry with the Woman (Our Lady) and went off to wage war against the rest of her offspring, those who keep God's commandments and bear witness to Jesus." Rev 12:17. Our Lady told Father Gobbi that we are living in this war today. She told him, "I am a Great Sign of battle between me and my Adversary, between the Woman and the Dragon, between my army and the army guided by the enemy of God. . . . It is necessary that all of you come as quickly as possible to form part of my army. For this, I again invite my children, to consecrate themselves to my Immaculate Heart and to entrust themselves to me as little children."

Our Lady told Marijna at Medjugorje, "You must know that Satan exists. One day, he presented himself before the throne of God and asked permission to try the Church for a period of time. God permitted him to try it during one century. This century is under the power of the devil, but when the secrets which have been confided to you have been fulfilled, his power will be destroyed."

To help us to realize the reality of Satan, Pope Paul VI said, "Evil is not merely a lack of something, but an affective agent, a living, spiritual being, perverted and perverting, a terrible reality." He said that "one of the greatest needs of the Church today is defense from that evil which is called the devil."

St. Maximillian Kolbe said that "modern times are dominated by Satan . . . . The conflict with hell cannot be engaged by man, even the most clever. The Immaculata alone has from God the promise of victory over Satan. However, assumed into heaven the Mother of God now requires our cooperation. She seeks souls who will consecrate themselves entirely to her who will become in her hands effective instruments for the defeat of Satan and the spreading of God's kingdom on earth." We are called to respond to Our Lady's call to join her army and engage in spiritual warfare through consecration, reparation and apostolic activity.

We should join her army by making the Total Consecration of St. Louis de Montfort and follow the example of the Holy Father who took as his papal motto *totus tuus* which means totally yours. He has totally consecrated himself, the Church and the world to her and recommends that we make our own personal Total Consecration. We should wear the Brown Scapular as a sign of our consecration by which we pay her homage, dedicate ourselves entirely to her service under her protection and imitate her virtues.

Our Lady of Fatima appeared in her last apparition as Our Lady of Mt. Carmel with a Brown Scapular hanging from her right hand. The Brown Scapular is an abbreviated form of the large scapular worn by the members of the Carmelite Order. Our Lady gave this scapular to St. Simon Stock in 1251 and promised, "Whosoever dies clothed in this shall never suffer eternal fire." This is the same promise of salvation that she promised at Fatima for those who embraced devotion to her Immaculate Heart. This is an effective motive for making the Total Consecration and wearing the Brown Scapular.

Our Lady told Father Gobbi, "Today there is need for a great force of prayer, there is need for a great chain of suffering, raised up to God in reparation." We should reparatively receive the Sacraments, pray and fast using Our Lady's weapons of the Rosary and Eucharistic adoration of the Blessed Sacrament. At Akita, Japan, Our Lady said, "The Only Arms which will remain for you will be the Rosary and the Sign left by my Son. Each day, recite the prayers of the Rosary. With the Rosary, pray for the Pope, the Bishops and the priests." We should pray together in cenacles, as Our Lady has requested, in order to receive the power of the Holy Spirit. Our Lady prayed with the Apostles in a cenacle and they received power from the Holy Spirit to courageously evangelize. See Acts 2:41. We should imitate them.

We should practice the First Saturday Devotion requested by Our Lady of Fatima to receive Holy Communion and Confession and pray five decades of the Rosary, together with fifteen minutes meditation on the mysteries, on five consecutive First Saturdays of the month with the intention of making reparation to the Immaculate Heart of Mary.

If possible, we should attend daily Mass; meditate on the daily Scripture readings and recite daily fifteen decades of the

Rosary. We should fast on bread and water on Wednesdays and Fridays if able; offer our sacrifices and sufferings in reparation for sins; lead an austere manner of life; practice the Christian virtues, especially purity, and be loyal and obedient to the Pope and the Bishops in union with him. In particular, we should obey the moral teachings of the Church in human sexuality, renounce sterilization and artificial contraception and learn natural family planning.

When we join Our Lady's army through our Total Consecration, use her reparative weapons and pray in cenacles, we are equipped for spiritual warfare and apostolic acitivity to end abortion. Our Lady told Father Gobbi, "You must be the apostles of these last times! . . . You have been chosen to combat courageously against the power of him who has placed himself in opposition to Christ in order to obtain in the end my greatest victory."

We should call upon the angels for help, give public witness at abortion killing centers and practice the spiritual and corporal works of mercy for the mothers of the unborn. We should charitably meet their needs, help them to bring their children to birth and mercifully receive those who have repented of their abortions. We should establish alternative Crisis Pregnancy houses near killing centers for the mothers who wish to seek immediate alternative help. We should go to the killing centers in public witness of our faith and prayerfully intercede for the mothers, their children and all who support the abomination of abortion. We should celebrate Memorial Masses for the aborted children, bury them and erect monuments to their memory. Let not Jesus say to us at the Judgment, "I was an unborn child and you forgot me." See Mt 25.

Cork, Ireland.
Youth Band.

Holy Rosary Parish, Phillipines.
Military Cadets.

Our Lady of Guadalupe,

Your Children

Welcome You!

Cebu, Phillipines.
Pre-Schoolers

San Francisco, California.
Indians at Mission Dolores Basilica.

Shown below is the left wall of the mosaic mural in the Chapel of Our Lady of Guadalupe in the National Shrine of the Immaculate Conception, Washington, D.C. Please see the explanation on the opposite page. This wall depicts pilgrims coming to venerate Our Lady of Guadalupe in Mexico from South America and Central America.

From the left are two Argentinian gauchos, a workman, St. Martin de Porres, a Bolivian woman, a Peruvian man, St. Mariana of Ecuador, a Guatemalan Mayan couple, an architect, St. Rose of Lima, a South American family, an Aztec chief, Sr. Juana Inez de la Crux, Hernan Cortes, Bishop Zumarraga and Juan Diego.

Who is she that comes forth like the rising dawn, fair as the moon, bright as the sun. Sg 6:10.

Like the rainbow gleaming amid luminous clouds, like the bloom of roses in the Spring. Sir 50:7-8.

These words are applied in the liturgy to Our Lady. They are inscribed on a mosaic mural located in Our Lady of Guadalupe Chapel in the National Shrine of the Immaculate Conception, Washington, D.C. The curved walls suggest the movement to Mexico of pilgrim peoples from all of the Americas to venerate Our Lady of Guadalupe, Patroness of the Americas. She is depicted above the Chapel altar.

The Chapel was designed by the Shrine architect, Eugene Kennedy, and the mosaic artist was Mary Reardon.

Please turn this page out to see the interior of the Chapel. The proportions of the images have been changed to fit these pages.

Piña Blanca, New Mexico. Fr. Donen Herbe

Manila, Phillipines. Cardinal Jaime Sin

Hail Holy Queen and Mother of the Americas!

Cebu, Phillipines. Crown and cascade of roses over Missionary Image.

Manila, Phillipines. Cardinal Roger Mahoney crowning Missionary Image before Cardinal Sin and two million of the Filipino faithful.

Japanese visionary Sister Agnes Sasagawa, victim-soul of Akita, being prayed over from left by Father Michael O'Carroll, author, Filipino priest and Simplicio Roxas, helper of the Marian Movement of Priests in the Philippines. Note Our Lady's pins worn by all.

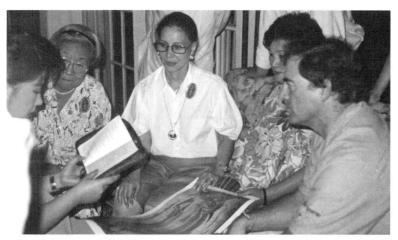

Korean visionary Julia Kim, victim-soul for abortion, with her translator who reads the Great Sign of Chapter 12 of the Book of Revelation. The author explains its correlation to an image of Our Lady of Guadalupe which is on Julia's lap. To the left of her is our Filipino hostess, Mercedes Tuason.

Praying for exorcism of the Red Dragon (see Rev 12) from abortion killing center in Oakland, California. Missionary Image apostolate twin workers, Janice Keen (left) and Joyce Keen kneel beside the Image.

Praying for exorcism of the Black Beast (see Rev 13) from Masonic Temple in Tulsa, Oklahoma. Note the book and Rosary.

25. Protectress of the Unborn, Queen and Mother of All Nations, Victorious Queen of Peace

Our Lady of Guadalupe recently promised, "Together, my dear children, we will end the horrible evil of abortion. I will help you stop all abortions. There will be no exceptions. Together we will bring about a new era of protecting all human life, that is, each person, from conception to natural death. I will put a stop to the present bloody human sacrifices like I did among the pagans after the miracle of my image began in 1531." See Appendix A, First Message.

Our Lady of Guadalupe appears in her image as a pregnant woman, signified by the sash tied above her womb, the four-petaled flower "Nahui Ollin" on her dress below the sash and as seen in her physiological appearance. Recent gynecological measurements have determined that Our Lady's image has the physical dimensions of a pregnant mother.

Our Lady also appears in the image of Chapter 12 of the Book of Revelation as the Woman Clothed with the Sun with the moon at her feet, pregnant with child. See Rev 12:1-2. She said to Juan Diego, "I will give all my protection to the people. I am the merciful mother of all mankind. . . . Am I not your fountain of *life*?" She came to Tepeyac to replace Tonantzin, the false mother goddess. She is a mother who protects her children from death.

We recall the promise of the *Memorare*, "Never was it known that anyone who fled to your protection was left unaided." Our Lady of Guadalupe recently said to "ponder well the promises of the Memorare." See Appendix A, Fifth Message. As Our Lady of Guadalupe ended human sacrifice in Mexico so she will also end human sacrifice by abortion. She acts as a mother who protects her unborn child from death. Therefore, she is commonly called the "Protectress of the Unborn." Cardinal Posadas referred to her under this title. See Appendix B.

When Pope John Paul II visited the Basilica of Our Lady of Guadalupe, he prayed to her, "Grant to our homes the grace of loving and respecting life in its beginnings, with the same love with which you conceived in your womb the life of the Son of God." See Appendix F. When he dedicated a chapel to Our Lady of Guadalupe on May 12, 1992 at St. Peter's Basilica in Rome, he prayed that she would "always defend the gift of life."

The popes have entitled Our Lady of Guadalupe as Patroness *and* Protectress of various geographic areas and peoples. The term "Patroness" implies a general overall care for the spiritual and material welfare of her clients while "Protectress" implies a particular aspect of that care. The title "Patroness and Protectress of the Unborn" is all-encompassing.

By this title we place under her patronage and protection the Pro-Life Movement and all unborn children. We beg her protection of the mothers of the unborn and the children within their wombs. We ask her to help these mothers to bring their children to birth and to save the souls of those who have been killed by abortion. This has been done on several occasions with the Missionary Image by an Act of Consecration and Crowning. See Appendix E.

Cardinal John O'Connor said, "We commend the Pro-Life Movement of the Archdiocese of New York to the protection and guidance of Our Lady of Guadalupe. . . . Our Lady of Guadalupe pray for America, pray for the Unborn." This fulfills her recent request to place the Pro-Life Movement under her banner. On her part she promised that "I will give you my powerful protection and help. I will lead you to victory over the forces of death which are preying upon babies in the wombs of their mothers." See Appendix A, First Message.

Many people wonder whether the unborn babies killed by abortion are saved? There is no definitive teaching by the Church on this issue. The Catechism of the Catholic Church (#1261) says that we are allowed to hope that God "may" save children who have died without Baptism. However, there is no specific reference to the unborn children killed by abortion.

Sacred Scripture tells us that "God our Savior wills everyone to be saved . . . ." 1 Tim 2:4. This may include the unborn children. So we hope that God may save them. The martyred Holy Innocents were saved by their Baptism of Blood. We trust that God may save the innocent aborted children by the Baptism of their Blood and our desire for their eternal salvation.

Our Lady told Father Gobbi of the Marian Movement of Priests with reference to them that "the love and anxiety of your heavenly Mother, *and of the Church*, for their salvation, with the innocent blood being spilled by those who despise and disobey the law of God, are a baptism of blood and desire saving all of them."

Our Lady told Julia Kim, the Korean mystic, that the aborted unborn are in a "limbo-like" state without suffering but that they are saved only by their blood *and* our desire and reparatory prayer and fasting. Their salvation is not automatic or assured. We must pray and sacrifice for their salvation so that they may receive the grace to choose God and be saved. We have hope and confidence in Our Lady of Guadalupe as Protectress of the Unborn that her love and anxiety for their salvation together with our help will save them. It has also been privately revealed that the aborted unborn pray for their mother's salvation.

Our Lady's first and foremost title given to her by her Son from the Cross is "Mother." See Jn 19:27. But because she is the Mother of the King she is also a Queen. See Lk 1:32.

She said to Juan Diego, "I am the Merciful Mother of all mankind." Therefore she is the Queen and Mother of All Nations.

Our Lady's Queenship was proclaimed by Pope Pius XII in his encyclical *Ad Caeli Reginam* in 1954. He said that "Mary has been made Queen of heaven and earth by God, exalted above all the choirs of angels and all the saints." He decreed that the Feast of her Queenship be celebrated on May 31st (now August 22nd). He established this day as the day on which the consecration of mankind to her Immaculate Heart is to be renewed. In a 1955 radio message to Fatima he said, "Jesus is King throughout all eternity by nature and by right of conquest. Through Him, with Him and subordinate to Him, Mary is Queen by grace, by divine relationship, by right of conquest, and by singular election."

So Our Lady's Queenship is equally extensive as the Kingship of her divine Son. It extends to all men and to all graces which are granted to men by her intercession and mediation as Queen and Mother of All Nations, Mediatrix of All Graces. Pope John Paul II prayed in his prayer to Mary for the Marian Year 1987, "To you, Mother of the human family *and of the nations*, we confidently entrust the whole of humanity."

Our Lady's Queenship reflects the characteristics of the Old Testament queens of Judah. The queen was not the king's wife but his *mother*. She occupied the throne at the right side of her son, had great influence upon him and a right to intervene in the king's affairs. See 1 Kgs 2:19. Our Lady intervened in her Son's affairs in Spain, in Mexico and from there as a River of Light to all nations.

God's first church was built at El Bethel. Our Lady's first miraculous intervention was at Zaragoza, Spain, where a church was built at her request. This was followed by her interventions and her churches at Guadalupe, Spain and Tepeyac, Mexico. A recent vision has connected these churches.

One day as John Bird was explaining his photograph of the tilma and the sword of light, a nun in the audience had a vision which appeared next to John. She later was able to paint this vision, although she was not an artist. It is entitled, *River of Light.*

This painting is shown at the end of this chapter. It symbolizes Our Lady of Guadalupe as the victorious Woman treading upon Satan, the serpent, in fulfillment of the promise of the Book of Genesis, chapter 3, verse 15. We see her as the River of Light standing within a vertical column of light over a river. She and the river have toppled and crushed the column of the stone serpent idol and replaced it with the column of the joyful mysteries of the Rosary at Tepeyac. "The people who walked in darkness have seen a great light; upon those who dwelt in the land of gloom a light has shown. You have brought them abundant joy and great rejoicing, . . . for the yoke that burdened them, the pole on their shoulder, and the rod of their taskmaster you have smashed . . . ." Is 9:1-3. Our Lady of Guadalupe mediated this light to the pagan Aztecs who dwelt in darkness. She brought them abundant joy and great rejoicing. She smashed the stone serpent idol and the yoke of human sacrifice that burdened them.

Our Lady of Guadalupe stands in the painting at the center of the columns from left to right, El Bethel, Zaragoza, Guadalupe and Tepeyac. El Bethel was the place chosen by God where the first shrine to the one true God was erected. Jacob exclaimed there, " 'Truly, the Lord is in this spot, although I did not know it!' In solemn wonder he cried out: 'How awesome is this shrine! This is nothing else but an abode of God, and that is the gateway to heaven!' Early the next morning, Jacob took the stone that he had put under his head, set it up as a memorial stone, and poured oil on top of it. He called that site Bethel.... ." Gn 28:16-19.

Zaragoza is the place of the first Christian church in the world. It is located in Spain. The site was chosen by Our Lady herself who bilocated there from Jerusalem. She appeared there to the apostle St. James, Evangelist of Spain, while she was still alive in the year 40 A.D. Our Lady asked St. James to build the first Catholic church there in her honor as she also later requested Juan Diego in Mexico to build a church for her there.

Guadalupe was also a Church chosen by Our Lady located in Spain. A statue of Our Lady, carved by St. Luke according to tradition, was buried there in 711 when the Moslems overran Spain. It was later discovered there when Our Lady appeared to a shepherd in 1328 and pointed it out to him. It was enshrined there by King Alfonso XI. Columbus and Cortes both made pilgrimages to Guadalupe before their voyages to the New World.

Tepeyac in Mexico was also a place chosen by Our Lady. Our Lady of Guadalupe personally appeared there, asked Juan Diego to have a church built there and today it welcomes more pilgrims then anywhere else in the entire world!

As we look at the painting, we see the angels of adoration and the passion watch over Our Lady of Guadalupe, River of Light. Our Lady told St. Mechtilde that the name Mary means "Lady of Light" because "God has filled me with wisdom and light, like a shining star, to light up heaven and earth." She told Bruno Cornacchiola at Tre Fontane, Italy, in 1946 that she was the Virgin of Revelation and the temple of the Holy Spirit.

Our Lady of Guadalupe is the ultimate temple connecting together the holy temples of God as the River of Light which has its source in Bethel, from which it flows through Zaragoza and Guadalupe to Tepeyac. From there it flows to the whole world in fulfillment of Pope John Paul II's prophecy that from the Basilica Shrine "the light of the Gospel of Christ will shine out over the whole world by means of the Miraculous Image of His Mother."

Our Lady's mission and power from the beginning as granted by God has been to crush the head of Satan. See Gn 3:15. She told Father Gobbi, "I am the victorious Woman. In the end, the power of Satan will be destroyed, and I myself will bind him with my chain and I will shut him up within his kingdom of death and of eternal torment, from which he will not be able to get out. In the world, there will reign the one and only conqueror of sin and of death, the king of the entire created universe, Jesus Christ."

Jesus has empowered us to help Our Lady to bring the victory and the triumph of her Immaculate Heart in the world today which will usher in His reign as Jesus King of All Nations. He said, "I have observed Satan fall like lightning from the sky. Behold, I have given you power to tread upon serpents and scorpions and upon the full force of the enemy and nothing will harm you." Lk 10:18-19.

We confidently await the era of peace that Our Lady promised us at Fatima in 1917.

We recall Pope Pius XII's expression of confidence in Our Lady of Guadalupe when he said, "We are certain that as long as you are recognized as Queen and as Mother, the Americas and Mexico will be safe."

We recall Our Lady of Guadalupe's promise to Juan Diego of giving her protection and her recent promise of "a new era of protecting all human life, that is, each person, from conception to natural death."

We rejoice in her promise to Father Gobbi, "My great victory against all the Masonic and Satanic forces will begin from here (the Basilica Shrine), for the greatest triumph of my Son Jesus.

I confirm to you that, by the Great Jubilee Year 2000, there will take place the Triumph of my Immaculate Heart, of which I foretold you at Fatima, and this will come to pass with the return of Jesus in glory, to establish His Reign in the world."

We respond to her invitation to Father Gobbi "to entrust yourselves to me, who am the Queen of Peace." We recall her promise to him of "a universal reign of grace, of beauty, of harmony, of communion, of sanctity, and justice and of peace."

Our Lady of Guadalupe Protectress of the Unborn
This painting shows Our Lady who protects her unborn children from the Red Dragon who voraciously seeks to devour them by abortion. See Rev 12:4.

Author with banner of Our Lady of Guadalupe, Protectress of the Unborn, at Akita International Marian Convention.

Our Lady of Guadalupe intercedes for the salvation of all souls, including the unborn, mercifully redeemed from Satan by the sacrifice of her Son.

River of Light. Painting of a vision which is explained in Chapter 25.

Author's wife, Sue, with Irish host Eammon O'Connor and Father Des O'Sullivan beneath the entrance to apparition site at Mellary Grotto, Ireland, with Our Lady's message to the world of PEACE AND PRAYER!

Contents

Appendices

APPENDIX A

OUR LADY OF GUADALUPE'S
RECENT MESSAGES

FIRST MESSAGE
August 14, 1990

I Am The Ever Virgin
Mother of The True God
Your Lady of Guadalupe

The miracle I began on 12 December 1531, at the geographical mid-point of the Americas, has continued without ceasing to the present time.

I gave you my image on the tilma worn by my faithful son, Juan Diego. My image, as Your Lady of Guadalupe, remains today as an ever active miracle; sustained by me for all to see.

However, I have been prematurely retired and restricted - not the reverent nor appropriate thing to do to the Woman Clothed with the Sun, your heavenly Mother.

My hands have been tied. I know it is love that has imprisoned me in that geographical mid-point of the Americas but it has kept me from my continuing mission, nevertheless.

If my image on Juan Diego's tilma was intended to bring only those 8-9 million people to my Son Jesus during the few years following 12 December 1531, why would I sustain the miracle of my image today, 459 years later?

Consider, for a moment, the possibility that I wanted to present my image for the sole benefit of those people during that short period of mass conversion and at most, no longer than the few years of life found naturally in the tilma's fibers. Would not the fiber and therefore the image itself have been reduced to only a small quantity of dust? Would not loving hands have protected that dust in an appropriate container, in a place of honor? That would have been continued in memory of a miracle I had performed for a certain time and a certain place, long ago.

But that is not the case.

I continue to sustain my miracle, even today.

I still want to be carried to my children throughout the land.

I want to travel throughout the length and breadth of the Americas.

My Son's Vicar on earth, Pope Pius XII, proclaimed me Empress of All the Americas and that I have predestined the Americas for a special purpose. Pope John XXIII proclaimed me as Queen of the Americas. Pope Benedict said of my image, "God and Mary have not performed such a marvelous deed for any other nation."

Once again, Your Lady of Guadalupe must move among all of my children in all of the Americas. Permit me, through the ever present and operative miracle of my image on Juan Diego's tilma, to bring many millions to my Son Jesus, through me.

I must be free to move about among my children so they may see me, their Mother, and come to her for comfort and help in these dark and dangerous times.

Release me from my present confinement with the same love that placed me here in this beautiful Mexican place of honor, respect and devotion.

I must be free to meet and turn all hearts in the Americas toward my Divine Son. I must be free to move among my children at will.

All of you must be my means of release and the means of my movement throughout the Americas.

I will melt your hearts with my motherly heart filled with love for you. I want you to give all your prayers, works, joys and sufferings with me, in me, through me and for me so that I may lead you safely to my Son Jesus.

As soon as you release me from my present captivity, located at the mid-point of the Americas, take me on a journey that will reach all states in the United States of America.

I want to stay, in a place of honor after that of my Son, at my beautiful National Shrine of the Immaculate Conception during the next week-long Rosary Congress.

Pray for my help in determining the route of my journey and the places where I will linger awhile. Do not hurry me, unnecessarily.

I want all of the Americas to prepare for my visit to the United States of America by prayer, fasting, confession and repentance of sin, taking part in the Holy Sacrifice of the Mass often, receiving my Son's Body and Blood in the Holy Eucharist often, adore Him in the Blessed Sacrament and prayerfully study Scripture and all of the teachings of the One, Holy, Catholic and Apostolic Church. Obey the teachings of the Magisterium, the Bishops in unity with my Son's Vicar on earth, Pope John Paul II. Pray my Rosary every day.

I want you to, immediately, place your entire pro-life force and efforts under my banner as Your Lady of Guadalupe. I will give you my powerful protection and help. I will lead you to victory over the forces of death which are preying upon babies in the wombs of their mothers.

Together, my dear children, we will end the horrible evil of abortion. I will help you stop all abortions. There will be no exceptions. Together we will bring about a new era of protecting all human life, that is, each person, from conception to natural death.

I will put a stop to the present bloody human sacrifices like I did among the pagans after the miracle of my image began in 1531.

In my image, you will see me as I want you to see me. In my image, as Your Lady of Guadalupe, there is no intermediary between you and me. There is no human seer needed as a go-between.

So few of you have noticed and given proper attention to my constant miracle going on before your eyes. My image is a continuing invitation to give yourselves to me so I may do with you what I have planned in bringing my children of all the Americas and the whole world to my Son Jesus through my Immaculate Heart.

Do not delay, now is the time, while I sustain my image for you.

I want to continue the mission I began in 1531.

Follow the example of my faithful son, Juan Diego, who has now been beatified by my first son on earth, Pope John Paul II, whom I have formed in my Immaculate Heart since he was a boy.

No third person or persons, seers, are relaying details of my appearance to you. You see with your own eyes, your Mother, Your Lady of Guadalupe. I want all my children to see me.

As you go forth under my banner, as Your Lady of Guadalupe, you will have no better guide than what my faithful son, St. Louis de Montfort, recommends as the True Devotion to me. Through this devotion, you will do all with me, in me, through me and for me as I lead you, as always to my Son Jesus and His Sacred Heart.

Please pray for and support my beloved priests in the Marian Movement of Priests.

I will send my angels to your side during all of your battles against the evil one and his works.

Coming to my shrine, in this captivity, inspired by your tender love for your Mother, is good. But recall how I came to Bishop Zumarraga through the miracle of my image. I did not wait for him to come to me on Tepeyac Hill. Recall, also, how I came to Juan Diego and even sought him when he tried to hide from me.

My appearances to Juan Diego (and to Juan Bernardino, Juan Diego's uncle) were made to them privately by me. They could tell others of my appearances to them but future events were needed to substantiate what they had told. In particular, Juan Diego, at first was an intermediary between me and Bishop Zumarraga.

Then, I revealed myself, through my image, directly to the Bishop and the others in the Bishop's house, at the time. These children of mine were only the first of all I want to see me in the Americas, until I take my image away.

The miracle of my image is intended for every man, woman and child, including babies in their mother's womb, for as long as I sustain my image among you.

Immediate preparation must be made for me, in my image, to travel all over the Americas so all will come and see me. Start my travels in the United States of America where my Divine Son Jesus is so neglected and rejected. Through the miracle of my image, I want to come among you and convert millions of your hearts to my Divine Son Jesus.

Am I not here? Am I not your Mother?

SECOND MESSAGE
October 17, 1990

I Am The Ever Virgin
Mother of The True God
Your Lady of Guadalupe

My Journey

You, my children, do not serve me and my request to travel throughout the width and breadth of the Americas by using worldly wisdom, logic, caution and a concern for human respect.

As obedient children, you will serve me by immediate actions based on complete trust in my motherly love and concern for you. You do your part and I will do mine. Together, we will overcome all obstacles to my journey. Stay close to me.

The time for my journey to begin is now, while I sustain the miracle of my image. I want millions to see my image, the Woman Clothed with the Sun. I will melt their hearts to conversion. Through my Immaculate Heart, I will lead them to the Sacred Heart of my Son.

Any hardship found along the path of my journey will be small compared to the joy of helping me bring millions of souls to my Son Jesus and His Holy Church.

My first son on earth, my Pope, John Paul II, will help you in all the ways that only he can accomplish through his office as the successor of Peter. Go to him. Listen to him. He represents my Son Jesus on earth, today.

Increase your prayers and fasting. Hasten your steps.

THIRD MESSAGE
October 30, 1990

I Am The Ever Virgin
Mother of The True God
Your Lady of Guadalupe

My Journey

My children, I know of your loving concern for the care and protection of my image during my travels throughout the Americas. With my motherly love, I look tenderly upon your concern. My journey is necessary so I will help you and comfort you in those concerns.

Follow what I, Your Lady of Guadalupe, told you to do in my other messages. Next, I want you to look to the Holy Family: the Infant Jesus, me and holy Joseph, my husband. Did not Joseph, in obedience to a message of an angel from God, protect my Baby, the Infant Jesus, and me from harm? Did he not protect us on our journey to and from Egypt? Holy Joseph will do the same for my journey throughout the Americas when you call upon him.

With the help of my Joseph and your own prudent care, my image will make the entire journey safely.

The safety of my image, the miracle I continue to sustain for you, my children, will be much greater traveling than it will be remaining at this geographical mid-point of the Americas against my wishes.

FOURTH MESSAGE
November 10, 1990

I Am The Ever Virgin
Mother of The True God
Your Lady of Guadalupe

Now that my previous three messages are being carried to many and my journey throughout the Americas is about to begin, I wish to gather you, my children, as one family for that journey. You who have searched for me, so lovingly, in many different directions and places, may now cease your search and join that family.

Am I not here in your Americas? Yes, I am here in the miracle of my image. I have sustained my miracle as a special gift for you, so necessary for you in these times.

Now, after 459 years, it is the time for me to begin my journey so all, in the Americas, may see me with their own eyes and know deeply the great love I have for each one of you, my children. You will have happen to you what happened to those millions of my children, one by one, so long ago.

Now that your search for me is over and you have found Your Lady of Guadalupe, give me the attention you have always wanted to give me, the Ever Virgin, the Mother of The True God. You, my children of the Americas, have a very special place in my plans for bringing all to the Sacred Heart of my Son Jesus through my Immaculate Heart. In my plan, the journey of my image throughout all of the Americas, is necessary. Prepare now. Do not delay. My children, you will not deny me, if you love me.

Give adoration and thanks to God. Pray My Rosary. Fast and do penance. Pray for one another. Support one another. Love one another. Pray for my Pope, my Bishops and my priests.

FIFTH MESSAGE
April 17, 1991

I Am the Ever Virgin
Mother of the True God
Your Lady of Guadalupe

My Journey

Today, I greet you my sons, Bishops of that land where I chose to leave my image on Juan Diego's tilma, so long ago, in 1531.

Recently, I had requested that you release my image from that mid-point of the Americas so it could travel freely; being a means I have chosen to convert millions of my children to my Son Jesus. You know of the millions of conversions following shortly after I gave my image and how human sacrifice stopped.

After thoughtful deliberation, you have judged that the release of my image cannot be permitted because of certain sensitivities involved. My sons, as the Magisterium in your land, your judgment will be obediently accepted by all who accept the authority my Son gave His Church.

As Queen and Mother of all the Americas, my concern for my poor wounded children grows greater in my Immaculate Heart every day. I want to reach them through my image. My sons, Bishops of Mexico, there is a way you can meet my request. My plan will require haste and much work on your part.

I request that you invite to my Shrine in Mexico City, the Bishops of all countries, territories and islands making up the Americas. Set the meeting on the Feasts of the Most Sacred Heart of Jesus and my Immaculate Heart.

Provide a replica of my image to the Bishops of each country, territory and island of the Americas. As the replicas travel their paths out from my image, those paths become rays of my love, care, protection and help for all my children everywhere. You my sons are responsible for making those paths which will become my promised special rays.

Invite my first son on earth, Pope John Paul II, who will bring unity and blessings needed for this my missionary work. Arrange ceremonies worthy of such a great and beautiful occasion.

To my sons, the Bishops of Mexico, who will extend the invitations and to my sons who will respond, I feel deeply how your flocks long for the care of their Shepherds.

Make haste! Did I, a young Virgin with Child, not make haste to the hill country to help my cousin Elizabeth? I expect no less response from you my sons to this crucial request that I make. Ponder well the promises of the Memorare.

SIXTH MESSAGE
April 28, 1992

I Am the Ever Virgin
Mother of the True God
Your Lady of Guadalupe

My children of the Americas, this is your earthly home. I came to your home, the Americas, for a special visit and for a special purpose, beginning in the year 1531.

It was then that I left a portrait, an image, of myself on the tilma of Juan Diego. In my great love and concern for all of you, I gave you visible proof of my special visit to your home, the Americas.

My special visit to your home will continue for as long as I sustain my image. Since 1531, and to this day, my faithful children have openly and with much affection greeted me, as a guest in their home, by the title of Our Lady of Guadalupe.

The special purpose I came to fulfill started over 460 years ago. From formerly worshipping the serpent-god, millions converted to the Catholic Church instituted by my Divine Son, Jesus Christ. During those early years the terrible practice of human sacrifice ended.

For many years, I was truly accepted, honored and my wishes were carried out. I was treated as a special guest in your home, the Americas.

My special visit continues. However, over time it began to be ignored and unnoticed. This grieves my Divine Son and me deeply. The special purpose I came to fulfill depends so much on your cooperation. You are a part of my plan. I knock softly and lovingly at the door of your heart. Please let me in.

You are in great need of my motherly love and protection. You and your home, the Americas, are being destroyed by pagan practices. Also, confusion is found even among you who want to lead good lives; even among you who search for me, the Mother of God. The distractions multiply. Please return to me, Your Lady of Guadalupe, with your whole heart and the gift of your hands for my work.

As a new reminder of my special visit to your home, the Americas, I have asked my sons, the Bishops of Mexico, to give a replica of my portrait on the tilma, as a Missionary Image, to each country, territory and island of your home, the Americas. My Missionary Image, given to the United States of the Americas, is now journeying across that land. Here, especially, the distractions turning you away from Your Lady of Guadalupe are many and strong. As I said to Juan Diego, on Tepeyac Hill, I say to you as Your Lady of Guadalupe, "Am I not your Mother? Do you need anything else?"

APPENDIX B
MEXICAN BISHOPS' AND BASILICA'S PRAYERS

Conference of All Mexican Bishops

The Conference of all Mexican Bishops in their plenary meeting, on their very first day, April 8, 1991, by means of the Archbishop of Guadalajara, Juan Jesus Posadas Ocampo, made the following prayers on petition of all of the Bishops:

"Mother of the True God, and our Mother, Our Lady of Guadalupe, we beg you that your trip through all the Americas be realized now beginning with the Marian Congress of the Rosary in the National Sanctuary of the Immaculate Conception in Washington, D.C., the next month of June. We know that you want to end abortion in the world and convert twenty-nine million Latins who have left the Church and have taken themselves over to the sects.

Lady, help us support your mission with our prayers in order that your Missionary Image will be well received in all the Americas."

Basilica of Our Lady of Guadalupe
OPEN LETTER TO THE CATHOLIC PEOPLE OF THE UNITED STATES

June the 14th, 1991

The Catholics of Mexico through me are sending you an image of Our Lady of Guadalupe.

It is not the original, but rather a Missionary Image which was stationed approximately twenty steps behind the original.

Our Lady wishes to use that image to help bring back to the Church of her Son the many millions of people who have left it.

At the same time Our Lady wishes to end the horrible crime of abortions.

We, in Mexico, offer our prayers to you attending the International Marian Congress of the Rosary in Washington, D.C.

In the name of the Abbot of the Basilica, Msgr. Guillermo Schulenburg, I remain,

s/ Msgr. Carlos Rogel
Pro-Vicario Episcopal

Basilica of Our Lady of Guadalupe

OPEN LETTER TO THE CATHOLIC PEOPLE OF THE UNITED STATES OF AMERICA

The Catholic people of Mexico through me give to the Catholic people of the United States of America, a Missionary Image of Our Lady of Guadalupe. It is an exact photographic replica of the original Miraculous Image located in the Basilica of Our Lady of Guadalupe. It was made to commemorate the 450th anniversary of her apparitions, December 12, 1981.

May Our Lady of Guadalupe fulfill the prophecy of Pope John Paul II made on that day that the Basilica will be a center "from which the light of the Gospel of Christ will shine out over the whole world by means of the Miraculous Image of His Mother."

The word Guadalupe in Spanish means "River of Light." May the Missionary Image of Our Lady of Guadalupe be a River of Light on her Journey throughout the United States. May she be well received and supported in her mission to end abortion and convert millions of hearts to the Sacred Heart of her Son Jesus and His holy Church through her Immaculate Heart!

May she, the Star of Evangelization be our hope!

I bless the Missionary Image and her evangelical mission.

s/ Msgr. Guillermo Schulenburg Prado
Abad de Guadalupe y
Vicario Episcopal

A Prayer for the
Missionary Image of Our Lady of Guadalupe

The Catholic people of Mexico and I pray to God that the paths of the Journey of the Missionary Image of Our Lady of Guadalupe throughout the United States of America, become rays of Our Lady's love, care, protection and help for all of her children, particularly the unborn.

May she end without exceptions the horrible evil of abortion.

May she convert millions of hearts to the Sacred Heart of her Son Jesus and His holy Church through her Immaculate Heart.

May all pro-life forces unite under the banner of Our Lady of Guadalupe with her title of "Protectress of the Unborn."

I bless the Missionary Image of Our Lady of Guadalupe and her evangelical mission that began under her protection almost 460 years ago.

I congratulate all the promoters of such a praiseworthy mission and with pleasure I commend them to the hands of Our Lord.

Lady, help us support your mission with our prayers in order that your Missionary Image may be well received in America for the glory of God and the honor of His holy Mother!

+ Juan Jesus Cardinal Posadas Ocampo
Archbishop of Guadalajara

Mexico, D.F., January 8, 1992

Dr. Daniel Lynch
St. Albans, Vermont

I greet you with best regards and wish you every good thing in the Lord.

I am happy to let you know that I received news of your apostolic work in the beloved country of the United States of America, where you promote knowledge and veneration of the Blessed Virgin of Guadalupe.

Your servant congratulates you and prays that the Virgin of Guadalupe bless your praiseworthy purposes.

In saying this, I am pleased to sign this letter with great affection, in Christ Jesus.

s/ ERNESTO CARDINAL CORRIPIO AHUMADA
Archbishop Primate of Mexico

Basilica of Our Lady of Guadalupe

September 30, 1992

This is to certify that any Image of Our Lady of Guadalupe bearing the signatures of Abbott Schulenburg of the Basilica and Cardinal Ernesto Corripio of Mexico is an authentic official reproduction of the original Image of Our Lady of Guadalupe.

Any person or group calling such Images fraudulent is committing a serious and grave falsehood.

We wish to assure you that Images bearing the above endorsements also contain our blessing.

s/ Msgr. Carlos Warnholtz
Basilica of Our Lady of Guadalupe

APPENDIX C

ST. LOUIS' ACT OF TOTAL CONSECRATION

Consecration to Jesus Christ,
the Incarnate Wisdom,
through the Blessed Virgin Mary

O Eternal and Incarnate Wisdom! O sweetest and most adorable Jesus! True God and true man, only Son of the Eternal Father, and of Mary, always Virgin! I adore Thee profoundly in the bosom and splendors of Thy Father during eternity; and I adore Thee also in the virginal bosom of Mary, Thy most worthy Mother, in the time of Thine Incarnation.

I give Thee thanks for that Thou hast annihilated Thyself, taking the form of a slave in order to rescue me from the cruel slavery of the devil. I praise and glorify Thee for that Thou has been pleased to submit Thyself to Mary, Thy holy Mother, in all things, in order to make me Thy faithful slave through her. But, alas, ungrateful and faithless as I have been, I have not kept the promises which I made so solemnly to Thee in my Baptism; I have not fulfilled my obligations; I do not deserve to be called Thy child, nor yet Thy slave; and as there is nothing in me which does not merit Thine anger and Thy repulse, I dare not come by myself before Thy most holy and august majesty. It is on this account that I have recourse to the intercession of Thy most holy Mother, whom Thou has given me for a mediatrix with Thee. It is through her that I hope to obtain of Thee contrition, the pardon of my sins, and the acquisition and preservation of wisdom.

Hail, then, O Immaculate Mary, living tabernacle of the Divinity, where the Eternal Wisdom willed to be hidden and to be adored by angels and by men! Hail, O Queen of Heaven and earth, to whose empire everything is subject which is under God. Hail, O sure refuge of sinners, whose mercy fails no one. Hear the desires which I have of the Divine Wisdom; and for that end receive the vows and offerings which in my lowliness I present to thee.

I (Name), a faithless sinner, renew and ratify today in thy hands the vows of my Baptism; I renounce forever Satan, his pomps and works; and I give myself entirely to Jesus Christ, the Incarnate Wisdom, to carry my cross after Him all the days of my life, and to be more faithful to Him than I have ever been before.

In the presence of all the heavenly court I choose thee this day for my Mother and Mistress. I deliver and consecrate to thee, as thy slave, my body and soul, my goods, both interior and exterior, and even the value of all my good actions, past, present and future; leaving to thee the entire and full right of disposing of me, and all that belongs to me, without exception, according to thy good pleasure, for the greater glory of God, in time and in eternity.

Receive, O benignant Virgin, this little offering of my slavery, in honor of, and in union with, that subjection which the Eternal Wisdom deigned to have to thy maternity, in homage to the power which both of you have over this poor sinner, and in thanksgiving for the privileges with which the Holy Trinity has favored thee. I declare that I wish henceforth, as thy true slave, to seek thy honor and to obey thee in all things.

O admirable Mother, present me to thy dear Son as His eternal slave, so that as He has redeemed me by thee, by thee He may receive me! O Mother of mercy, grant me the grace to obtain the true Wisdom of God; and for that end receive me among those who thou lovest and teachest, whom thou leadest, nourishest and protectest as thy children and thy slaves.

O faithful Virgin, make me in all things so perfect a disciple, imitator and slave of the Incarnate Wisdom, Jesus Christ thy Son, that I may attain, by thine intercession and by thine example, to the fullness of His age on earth and of His glory in Heaven. Amen.

APPENDIX D

ACT OF CONSECRATION OF GUARDIANS OF LIFE TO OUR LADY OF GUADALUPE PROTECTRESS OF THE UNBORN

Our Lady of Guadalupe, Ever Virgin, Mother of the True God, Woman Clothed with the Sun, I totally consecrate myself to you and to your Sorrowful and Immaculate Heart.

In humility, through this consecration, I receive you, Virgin of Guadalupe, into every moment of my life and every fiber of my being. I am assured that God has chosen you for me and recall what the Angel of the Lord told St. Joseph: "Do not be afraid to take Mary to yourself because what is in her is of the Holy Spirit." Mt 1:20.

Holy Archangel Gabriel who presented to us the beauty and virtues of Mary's soul, (see Lk 1:26-35) obtain for me the grace to imitate these virtues and, by my example, to show others how to live, how to love, how to sacrifice and how to die.

As I receive you, Queen and Mother of the Americas, I desire, with your help, to grow in my relationship with you, a relationship which was established by your Divine Son as He hung dying on the Cross when He said to you His Holy and Sorrowful Mother, "Woman, behold your Son!" and to St. John, the beloved disciple, "Son, behold your Mother!" Jn 19:26-27.

I consecrate to you, Protectress of the Unborn, my work of protecting the sacredness of all human life from conception to natural death; my work in spreading the Good News; and my work in renewing and protecting the sanctity of the family. I ask for the special protection of the Infant Jesus, of you His Mother and of St. Joseph, guardian of the Holy Family of Nazareth.

I implore you, Queen of the Angels, to send St. Michael and the other angels to defend us in our battle against Satan and all of the evil spirits in this present darkness arrayed against God and the human life He creates. See Eph 6:12.

In reparation I will pray and sacrifice. Please pray for us who seek refuge in you, for the conversion of poor sinners who offend you and for the salvation of all souls!

I promise to keep ever before me your instructions at the Wedding Feast at Cana, "Do whatever He tells you." Jn 2:5. In doing so, I will be loyal and obedient to the Pope, your first son on earth. I am sure in my consecration to you that you will lead me on a safe and sure path to the Sacred Heart of Jesus.

Holy Mother of God, save us through the Flame of Love of your Sorrowful and Immaculate Heart! Send forth the grace from your Flame of Love to the whole human race now and at the hour of our death. Send forth your Spouse, the Holy Spirit, to bring us the New Pentecost and the fire of His Divine Love to renew the face of the earth.

Let there be revealed, once more, in the history of the world the infinite power of merciful love. May it put an end to evil. May it transform consciences. May your Sorrowful and Immaculate Heart reveal for all the light of hope. May Jesus King of All Nations reign in our hearts, our families, cities, states, nations and the whole of humanity. May His reign be recognized on earth!

O clement, O loving, O Sweet Virgin Mary, hear our pleas and accept this cry from our hearts!

Dear Lady of Guadalupe, I conclude my consecration to you with the message you gave to Blessed Juan Diego in Mexico on Tepeyac Hill in 1531 hereby accepting it also as a message from you to me.

Know for certain that I am the perfect and perpetual Virgin Mary, Mother of the True God. . . . Here I will show and offer all my love, my compassion, my help and my protection to the people. I am your merciful Mother, the Mother of all those who love me, of those who cry to me, of those who have confidence in me. Here I will hear their weeping and their sorrows and will remedy and alleviate their sufferings, necessities and misfortunes. . . . Listen and let it penetrate into your heart. . . . Do not be troubled or weighed down with grief. Do not fear any illness or vexation, anxiety or pain. Am I not here who am your Mother? Are you not under my shadow and protection? Am I not your fountain of life? Are you not in the folds of my mantle? In the crossing of my arms? Is there anything else that you need?

APPENDIX E

ACT OF CONSECRATION AND CROWNING TO OUR LADY OF GUADALUPE PATRONESS AND PROTECTRESS OF THE UNBORN

Our Lady of Guadalupe, Immaculate Conception, Perfect and Perpetual Virgin Mary, Mother of the True God and Mother of the Church, Woman Clothed with the Sun, we totally consecrate ourselves to you and to your Sorrowful and Immaculate Heart. We entrust to you all that we have and all that we are. Hear the prayer that we address to you with filial trust and present it to your son Jesus, our sole Redeemer.

As the Immaculate Conception, you are the Patroness of America. Our Holy Fathers have called you Patroness, Queen and Mother of the Americas. Popes Leo XIII and Pius XII crowned your sacred image at Tepeyac.

Today we imitate them and address you, Our Lady of Guadalupe, as our Patroness, our Queen and our Mother and we crown your Missionary Image.

We place under your patronage and protection the Pro-Life Movement and all unborn children under your special title of Patroness and Protectress of the Unborn. Please protect all mothers of the unborn and the children within their wombs. Please help their mothers to bring them to birth and help to save the souls of those who have been killed by abortion.

O Mother of Mercy, help all abortionists and abortion supporters to be healed and reconciled with your Son. Melt hearts so that life may be revered from conception to natural death. Bring us the new era of reverence for life. We pledge to help you with our prayer and sacrifice. Please end the horrible evil of the abortion holocaust without exceptions now!

We implore you, Queen of the Angels to defend all of your children and to send St. Michael and the other angels to defend us in our battle against Satan and all of the evil spirits in this present darkness arrayed against God and the human life He creates. See Eph 6:12.

Holy Mother of God, Mediatrix of All Graces, save us through the Flame of Love of your Sorrowful and Immaculate Heart! Send forth the grace from your Flame of Love to the whole human race now and at the hour of our death. Send forth your Spouse, the Holy Spirit, to bring us the New Pentecost and the fire of His Divine Love to renew the face of the earth.

We desire that the innocent unborn children who die without Baptism should be baptized and saved. We ask that you obtain this grace for them and repentance, reconciliation and pardon from God for their parents and their killers.

Let there be revealed, once more, in the history of the world the infinite power of merciful love. May it put an end to evil. May it transform consciences. May your Sorrowful and Immaculate Heart reveal for all the light of hope. May Jesus King of All Nations reign in our hearts, our families, cities, states, nations and the whole of humanity. May His reign be recognized on earth!

O clement, O loving, O sweet Virgin Mary, hear our pleas and accept this cry from our hearts!

Our Lady of Guadalupe, Patroness and Protectress of the Unborn, pray for us!

We place above your head, this crown as a sign of your Queenship. You reign as Queen with your Son Jesus, King of All Nations. May this coronation be received by you, O humble Virgin Mother, so that you will reign in the hearts of all mothers. This crown puts forever under your powerful patronage and protection all unborn children and their mothers, under your title as Patroness and Protectress of the Unborn.

Long live Our Lady of Guadalupe, Patroness and Protectress of the Unborn!

APPENDIX F

PRAYERS TO OUR LADY OF GUADALUPE COMPOSED BY POPES

On October 12, 1945, Pope Pius XII re-crowned the Miraculous Image of Our Lady of Guadalupe which was first crowned in 1895 by Pope Leo XIII. In his radio address he prayed:

> Hail, Fount most abundant from which springs the streams of Divine Wisdom, repelling with the most pure and limpid waters of orthodoxy, the turbulent waves of error. Hail, O Virgin of Guadalupe, Empress of America and Queen of Mexico, we to whom the admirable ordering of Divine Providence has confided - without taking into consideration our unworthiness - the sacred treasure of Divine Wisdom on earth, for the salvation of all souls, place again today above your brow the crown, which puts forever under your powerful patronage the purity and the integrity of the holy faith in Mexico and in all the American continents. For we are certain that as long as you are recognized as Queen and as Mother, the Americas and Mexico will be safe.

On October 12, 1961, Pope John XXIII gave a radio address on the occasion of the solemn closing of a year dedicated to Our Lady of Guadalupe. He prayed:

> Hail Mother of the Americas, Heavenly Missionary of the New World! From the Sanctuary of Tepeyac you have been for more than four centuries the Mother and Teacher of the Faith to the peoples of the Americas. Be also our protection and save us, O Immaculate Mary. Aid our rulers. Stir up a new zeal in our prelates. Increase the virtues of our clergy, and preserve forever our Faith. In every home may the holiness of the family flourish, and in the shelter of the home may Catholic education, favored by your own benign glance, achieve a wholesome growth. Amen.

On November 20, 1962 in Our Lady of Guadalupe Church, Rome, Pope John XXIII prayed:

Our Lady of Guadalupe, you who have desired to give special signs of benevolence to the land of Mexico and have promised consolation and help to those who love you and follow you, gaze kindly on all of your children. They invoke you with confidence.

Preserve in our souls the precious gift of divine grace. Make us docile to the will of Our Lord in such a manner that His reign may be extended more and more in our hearts, in our families and in our beloved nation.

O most holy Virgin, be with us in the fatigues of our daily work, in the joys as well as in the pains and difficulties of life, so that our immortal spirit may rise, free and pure, to God, and that we may serve Him joyfully with generosity and fervor.

Defend us from all evil, O Queen and Mother of Mexico, and make us faithful imitators of your Divine Son, Jesus, who is the Way, the Truth, and the Life, so that one day, guided by your hand, we may reach the reward of the beatific vision in heaven. Amen.

On January 27, 1979, Pope John Paul II celebrated Mass in the New Basilica. It was his first pilgrimage as Pope and the first time that a Pope had visited the Guadalupe Shrine. He prayed:

O, Immaculate Virgin, Mother of the true God and Mother of the Church! You, who from this place reveal your clemency and your pity to all those who ask for your protection; hear the prayer that we address to you with filial trust, and present it to your Son Jesus, our sole Redeemer.

Mother of Mercy, Teacher of hidden and silent sacrifice - to you, who come to meet us sinners - we dedicate on this day all our being and all our love.

We also dedicate to you our life, our work, our joys, our infirmities and our sorrows.

Grant peace, justice and prosperity to our peoples; for we entrust to your care all that we have and all that we are, Our Lady and Mother.

We wish to be entirely yours and to walk with you along the way of complete faithfulness to Jesus Christ in His Church.

Hold us always with your loving hand.

Virgin of Guadalupe, Mother of the Americas, we pray to you for all the Bishops, that they may lead the faithful along paths of intense Christian life, of love and humble service of God and souls.

Contemplate this immense harvest, and intercede with the Lord that He may instill a hunger for holiness in the whole People of God, and grant abundant vocations of priests and religious, strong in the faith and zealous dispensers of God's mysteries.

Grant to our homes the grace of loving and respecting life in its beginnings, with the same love with which you conceived in your womb the life of the Son of God.

Blessed Virgin Mary, Mother of Fair Love, protect our families, so that they may always be united, and bless the upbringing of our children.

Our hope, look upon us with compassion, teach us to go continually to Jesus and, if we fail, help us to rise again, to return to Him, by means of the confession of our faults and sins in the Sacrament of Penance, which gives peace to the soul.

We beg you to grant us a great love for all the holy Sacraments, which are, as it were, the signs that your Son left us on earth.

Thus, Most Holy Mother, with the peace of God in our conscience, with our hearts free from evil and hatred, we will be able to bring to all, true joy and true peace, which come to us from your Son, our Lord Jesus Christ, who with God the Father and the Holy Spirit, lives and reigns forever and ever. Amen.

APPENDIX G

POPE LEO XIII's PRAYER OF EXORCISM

THE FOLLOWING CAN BE READ IN UNISON WITH A LEADER AT ABORTION KILLING CENTERS. YOU SHOULD HAVE THERE WITH YOU A CRUCIFIX, HOLY WATER, BLESSED SALT AND AN IMAGE OF OUR LADY OF GUADALUPE.

Prayer Against Satan
and
The Rebellious Angels

Published by order of
His Holiness, Pope Leo XIII.

In the Name of the Father, and of the Son, and of the Holy Spirit. Amen.

Prayer to Saint Michael the Archangel

Most glorious prince of the heavenly armies, Saint Michael the Archangel, defend us in "our battle against principalities and powers, against the rulers of this world of darkness, against the spirits of wickedness in the high places." (Eph 6:12). Come to our assistance whom God has created to His likeness and whom He has redeemed at a great price from the tyranny of the devil. Holy Church venerates you as her guardian and protector; to you the Lord has entrusted the souls of the redeemed to be led into heaven. Pray therefore that the God of Peace will crush Satan beneath our feet, that he may no longer retain us captive and do injury to the Church. Offer our prayers to the Most High, that without delay they may draw His mercy down upon us. Take hold of "the Dragon, the old Serpent, which is the Devil and Satan," bind him and cast him into the bottomless pit so that he may no longer seduce the nations. (See Rev 20:2).

Exorcism

In the Name of Jesus Christ, our Lord and God, strengthened by the intercession of the Immaculate Virgin Mary, Mother of God, of Blessed Michael the Archangel, of the Blessed Apostles Peter and Paul and all the saints, we confidently undertake to repulse the attacks and deceits of the devil.

God arises. His enemies are scattered and those who hate Him flee before Him.

As smoke is driven away, so are they driven, as wax melts before the fire, so the wicked perish at the presence of God. *(Here Leader holds up the Cross).*

V. Behold the Cross of the Lord! Flee, bands of enemies.

R. He has conquered, the Lion of the tribe of Judah, the offspring of David.

V. May your mercy, Lord, descend upon us.

R. As great as our hope in you.

(The crosses indicate the Sign of the Cross to be made silently by all).

We drive you from us, whoever you may be, unclean spirits, all satanic powers, all infernal invaders, all wicked legions, assemblies and sects. In the Name and by the power of Our Lord Jesus Christ, † may you be snatched away and driven from the Church of God and from the souls made to the image and likeness of God and redeemed by the Precious Blood of the Divine Lamb. † Most cunning serpent, you shall no more dare to deceive the human race, persecute the Church, torment God's elect and sift them as wheat. † The Most High God commands you, † He with whom, in your great insolence, you still claim to be equal; "He who wants all men to be saved and to come to the knowledge of the truth." (I Tim 2:4). God the Father commands you. † God the Son commands you. † God the Holy Spirit commands you. † Christ, God's Word made flesh, commands you; † He who to save our race outdone through your envy, "humbled Himself, becoming obedient even unto death" (Phil 2:8); He who has built His Church on the firm rock and declared that the gates of hell shall not prevail against her, because He will dwell with her "all days even to the end of the world." (Mt 28:20). The sacred Sign of the Cross commands you, † as does also the power of the mysteries of the Christian Faith. † The glorious Mother of God, the Virgin Mary, commands you; † She who by her humility and from the first moment of her Immaculate Conception, crushed your proud head. The faith of the Holy Apostles Peter and Paul and of the other Apostles commands you. † The blood of the Martyrs and the pious intercession of all the Saints command you. †

Thus, cursed dragon, and you, diabolical legions, we adjure you by the living God, † by the true God, † by the holy God, † by the God "who so loved the world that He gave up His only Son, that every soul believing in Him might not perish but have life everlasting" (Jn 3:16), stop deceiving human creatures and pouring out to them the poison of eternal damnation; stop harming the Church and hindering her liberty. Begone, Satan, inventor and master of all deceit, enemy of our salvation. Give place to Christ in whom you have found none of your works; give place to the One, Holy, Catholic and Apostolic Church acquired by Christ at the price of His Blood. Stoop beneath the all-powerful hand of God; tremble and flee when we invoke the holy and terrible name of Jesus, this Name which causes hell to tremble, this Name to which the Virtues, Powers and Dominations of heaven are humbly submissive, this Name which the Cherubim and Seraphim praise unceasingly repeating: Holy, holy, holy is the Lord, the God of armies.

V. O Lord, hear my prayer.
R. And let my cry come unto you.
V. May the Lord be with you.
R. And with your spirit.

Let us Pray

God of heaven, God of earth, God of Angels, God of Archangels, God of Patriarchs, God of Prophets, God of Apostles, God of Martyrs, God of Confessors, God of Virgins, God who has power to give life after death and rest after work, because there is no other God than you and there can be no other, for you are the Creator of all things, visible and invisible, of whose reign there shall be no end, we humbly prostrate ourselves before your glorious majesty and we beseech you to deliver us by your power from all the tyranny of the infernal spirits, from their snares, their lies and their furious wickedness; deign, O Lord, to grant us your powerful protection and to keep us safe and sound. We beseech you through Jesus Christ our Lord. Amen.

From the snares of the devil, deliver us, O Lord.

That your Church may serve you in peace and liberty, we beseech you to hear us.

That you may crush down all enemies of your Church, we beseech you to hear us.

Ritual of Holy Water and Salt

(Holy water is now sprinkled at the killing center by the Leader while all pray):

Eternal Father, may this holy water that we sprinkle turn aside every attack of the unclean spirit and dispel the terror of the poisonous serpent from this killing center. In your mercy make the Holy Spirit present here and bring true health and protection and care for life, through our Lord Jesus Christ, your Son, who lives and reigns with you in the unity of the same Holy Spirit, one God, forever and ever. Amen.

(Salt is now sprinkled by the Leader on a line across the entranceways to the killing center while all pray):

Eternal Father, you ordered salt to be poured into the water by Elijah in order to restore its life-giving powers. We pour this blessed salt onto this land which you created in order to restore its use for life-giving and to prevent its use for the killing of the innocent unborn. May no one cross this line of salt for purposes of killing. May it be a barricade to abortionists, their supporters and mothers who seek abortion. May it put to flight and drive away from this killing center every apparition, every villainy and turn of devilish deceit and every unclean spirit adjured by your Son, Jesus Christ, who will come to judge the living and the dead and the world by fire, who lives and reigns with you in the unity of the Holy Spirit, one God forever and ever. Amen.

St. Michael's Prayer

St. Michael the Archangel defend us in Battle, be our protection against the wickedness and snares of the devil. May God rebuke him, we humbly pray and do you, O Prince of the Heavenly Host, by the Divine Power of God, cast into hell Satan and all of the other evil spirits who prowl about the world seeking the ruin of souls. Amen.

APPENDIX H

PRAYER FOR ABORTION VICTIMS TO THE SORROWFUL AND IMMACULATE HEART OF MARY, OUR LADY OF GUADALUPE, PROTECTRESS OF THE UNBORN

Jesus told an American mystic to "pray for all those who have been involved in abortions. Yes, pray that they become reconciled with Me. Many stay away out of pride. Others do not return to Me for Satan has them bound by fear and guilt. But my arms are outstretched and filled with love and mercy. Pray that these souls are healed emotionally and spiritually. Pray for any who encourage abortion, or aid in the act itself. These too, my mercy calls. Many who submit to this heinous crime are being misled. Pray that hearts open to the truth."

And so we pray for all victims of abortion. May those involved in abortions be reconciled to God and may the innocent dead be saved.

(If prayed at a killing center, all who are able should now KNEEL.)

Holy Mother of God and of the Church, Our Lady of Guadalupe, you were chosen by the Father for the Son through the Holy Spirit.

You are the Woman through whom Satan is crushed. (See Gen 3:15). You are the Woman Clothed with the Sun who labors to give birth to the Body of Christ while Satan, the Red Dragon, waits to voraciously devour your child. (See Rev 12).

So too did Herod seek to voraciously destroy your Son, Our Lord and Savior Jesus Christ, and massacred many innocent children in the process. (See Mt 2).

So today abortion killing centers massacre many innocent unborn children and exploit many mothers in an attack upon human life and upon the Church, the Body of Christ.

Like Rachel, we lament and we bewail the children who are no more. (See Mt 2:18).

Mother of the Innocents, we praise God in you for His gifts to you of your Immaculate Conception (conceived without original sin), your freedom from actual sin; your fullness of grace, your Motherhood of God and of the Church, your Perpetual Virginity and your Assumption body and soul into heaven.

To your Sorrowful and Immaculate Heart we pray for all killing centers throughout the world. We ask you to intercede with God to convert killing centers to centers that protect and foster all human life, married life and the family, God's foundation for society.

We place under your patronage and protection the Pro-Life Movement and all unborn children under your special title of Patroness and Protectress of the Unborn. Please protect all mothers of the unborn and the children within their wombs. Please help their mothers to bring them to birth and help to save the souls of those who have been killed by abortion.

O Mother of Mercy, help all abortionists and abortion supporters to be healed and reconciled with your Son. Melt hearts so that life may be revered from conception to natural death. Bring us the new era of reverence for life. We pledge to help you with our prayer and sacrifice. Please end the horrible evil of the abortion holocaust without exceptions now!

We implore you, Queen of the Angels to defend all of your children and to send St. Michael and the other angels to defend us in our battle against Satan and all of the evil spirits in this present darkness arrayed against God and the human life He creates. (See Eph 6:12).

Holy Mother of God, Mediatrix of All Graces, save us through the Flame of Love of your Sorrowful and Immaculate Heart! Send forth the grace from your Flame of Love to the whole human race now and at the hour of our death. Send forth your Spouse, the Holy Spirit, to bring us the New Pentecost and the fire of His Divine Love to renew the face of the earth.

We desire that the innocent unborn children who die without Baptism should be baptized and saved. We ask that you obtain this grace for them and repentance, reconciliation and pardon from God for their parents and their killers.

Let there be revealed, once more, in the history of the world the infinite power of Merciful Love. May it put an end to evil. May it transform consciences. May your Sorrowful and Immaculate Heart reveal for all the light of hope. May Jesus King of All Nations reign in our hearts, our families, cities, states, nations and the whole of humanity. May His reign be recognized on earth!

O clement, O loving, O sweet Virgin Mary, hear our pleas and accept this cry from our hearts!

APPENDIX I

PRAYER FOR RUSSIA

(This prayer was printed in Russian on the reverse side of an image of Our Lady of Guadalupe).

This is Mary, OUR LADY OF GUADALUPE, Mother of Our Lord and Savior Jesus Christ. She left her Miraculous Image on the cloak of Blessed Juan Diego, an Aztec Indian, on December 12, 1531 in Mexico. She ended human sacrifice and converted 10 million Indians to the One True Catholic Church in the next ten years!

Pope John Paul II prophesied that "the light of the Gospel of Christ will shine out over the whole world by means of the Miraculous Image of his Mother."

Our Lady of Guadalupe is the Woman Clothed with the Sun with the moon at her feet (See Rev 12:1) and the Woman who will crush the proud head of Satan. (See Gn 3:15). She has crushed the proud head of the Red Dragon of atheistic Communism and will soon end human sacrifice by abortion and crush the proud head of the Black Beast of Freemasonry. (See Rev 12, 13).

O Immaculate Conception, Our Lady of Guadalupe, Queen and Mother of All Nations look down upon this distressed and suffering world. You know our misery and our weakness. O you who are our Mother saving us in the hour of danger, have pity on us in these days of great and heavy trial.

Jesus has confided to you the treasure of His grace and through you He wishes to grant us pardon and mercy. In these hours of anguish your children come to you as their hope. We recognize your Queenship and ardently desire the triumph of your Immaculate Heart, the unity of the Church and the era of peace for mankind. May Russia glorify the Church!

We need a mother and a mother's heart. You are for us the bright dawn which scatters the darkness and points out the way to life. In your mercy obtain for us the hope and confidence of which we have such need.

Most holy and adorable Trinity you have crowned with glory in heaven the Blessed Virgin Mary Mother of the Savior. Grant that all her children on earth may recognize her as their Sovereign Queen and that all hearts, homes and nations may recognize her reign and her rights as Queen and Mother of All Nations who reigns both now and forever with her Son Jesus, King of All Nations.

HAVE FAITH AND BE CONVERTED TO JESUS CHRIST AND HIS CHURCH! PRAY AND FAST FOR PEACE!

APPENDIX J

MEMORARE OF ST. BERNARD

Remember, most gracious Virgin Mary, that never was it known that anyone who fled to your protection, implored your help or sought your intercession, was left unaided.

Inspired by this confidence, we fly unto you, O Virgin of virgins, our Mother. To you do we come, before you we stand, sinful and sorrowful. O Mother of the Word Incarnate, despise not our petitions, but in your mercy hear and answer them. Amen.

APPENDIX K

MEMORARE TO OUR LADY OF GUADALUPE

Remember, O most gracious Virgin of Guadalupe, that in your celestial apparitions on the mount of Tepeyac, you promised to show your compassion and pity towards all who, loving and trusting you, seek your help and call upon you in their necessities and afflictions. You promised to hear our supplications, to dry our tears and to give us consolation and relief. Never has it been known that anyone who fled to your protection, implored your help, or sought your intercession, either for the common welfare, or in personal anxieties, was left unaided.

Inspired by this confidence, we fly unto you, O Mary, ever Virgin Mother of the true God! Though grieving under the weight of our sins, we come to prostrate ourselves in your august presence, certain that you will deign to fulfill your merciful promises. We are full of hope that, standing beneath your shadow and protection, nothing will trouble or afflict us, nor need we fear illness or misfortune, or other sorrow.

You have desired to remain with us through your admirable Image, you who are our Mother, our health and our life. Placing ourselves beneath your maternal gaze and having recourse to you in all our necessities, we need do nothing more.

O holy Mother of God, despise not our petitions, but in your mercy hear and answer them. Amen.

APPENDIX L

THE CHAPLET OF OUR LADY OF GUADALUPE

This 24 bead Chaplet consists of six units of a single bead and a group of three beads. The six single beads signify the six apparitions of Our Lady of Guadalupe.

Make the sign of the Cross and say the Apostles' Creed. Say one "Our Father," three "Hail Marys" and one "Glory Be."

Announce the first apparition listed below and say one "Our Father," three "Hail Marys" and one "Glory Be." Repeat for each apparition. At the end say the Closing Prayer.

1st Apparition: Our Lady of Guadalupe appears to Blessed Juan Diego on Tepeyac Hill and requests that a temple be built there in her honor.

2nd Apparition: Our Lady of Guadalupe gives Juan encouragement to continue his mission after his first return from the Bishop's house.

3rd Apparition: Our Lady of Guadalupe promises Juan a sign for the Bishop after his second return from the Bishop's house.

4th Apparition: Our Lady of Guadalupe appears to Juan's uncle, Juan Bernardino, and he is healed and restored to health.

5th Apparition: Our Lady of Guadalupe asks Juan to pick the Castilian roses blooming on Tepeyac Hill and arranges them in his tilma.

6th Apparition: Our Lady of Guadalupe fulfills her promise to Juan by showing herself on his tilma to the Bishop.

Closing Prayer: Praised be the name of Jesus. May you the Virgin of Guadalupe, the Mother of the true God, help all those who invoke you to help with their necessities. May you guide us in righteous paths and protect us from all evil. Long live Christ the King! Long live Our Lady of Guadalupe! Amen.

APPENDIX M
MAKE OF ME A TILMA
Patti Gallagher Mansfield

O Most Holy Lord, You can do all things.

Make of me a tilma,
To show forth your love to the peoples of the New World you caused the image of your Merciful Mother to appear on the cloak of Juan Diego long ago.

If this rough-hewn fabric could attract your attention and be useful in your plan,

Surely a willing soul like mine can serve your purpose as well.

Make of me a tilma,
Take from me all that would spoil or distort the work of your hand.

May your Holy Spirit render me clean and ready to receive so great a gift.

Impress upon me the image of your pure and holy Mother,

May her countenance, her presence, her love be indelibly stamped upon me.

Make of me a tilma,
In this time when pagan culture threatens to engulf your people once more and destroy human life,

Let there be a fresh miracle of grace.

Send your Mother for a new evangelization.

Upon the coarse fabric of my life, draw this portrait so pleasing to You . . .

The image of Mary . . . the one who bears and brings forth Jesus.

May this beautiful Woman, clothed with the sun, live out her triumph in me . . .

Crushing the Serpent, radiating your mercy, and leading to faith all those who gaze upon her.

Yes, Lord, Make of me a tilma,
Amen.

© October 1992 Patti Gallagher Mansfield
On the Fifth Centenary of the Evangelization of the New World
Reprinted with permission

APPENDIX N
SONGS TO OUR LADY OF GUADALUPE
SONG TO OUR MOTHER
Sung by Indian Pilgrims

At the foot of the hill
Where the roses bloomed
I contemplate the Virgin
Who captured my heart.

Mother mine of Guadalupe
Mother mine, all love,
We beg you to give us
Your benediction and peace.

No other nation on earth
Has been so blessed by God
For that the Indians of Mexico
Carry you in their hearts.

Guadalupe, Guadalupe,
The name that brings us joy,
May it be ever on our lips
With great devotion.

May you be praised in heaven
Sweet Virgin Mother of God
And on earth beloved
From end to end of our land.

On Tepeyac she appeared
Like a divine Star
She is there to be our light
To protect and guide us.

Glory to the Immortal Princess
Who freed us from great evil
And to make us happy
She crushed the serpent.

Guadalupe, Guadalupe,
The name that brings us solace
It's the name of my Mother,
Of my Mother and of God's.

SONG TO OUR LADY OF GUADALUPE
Sung by Indian Pilgrims

With delight I have seen the opening of perfumed flowers
In your presence, Holy Mary.

Beside the still waters, I have heard Holy Mary singing:
I am the precious plant with hidden buds;
I was created by the One and Perfect God;
I am supreme among His creatures.

O Holy Mary, you live again in your picture.
And we, the lords of this land
Sing all together from the book of anthems,
In perfect harmony we dance before you.
And you, our Bishop, our Father, preached
Over there, by the lake side.

In the beauty of the flowers did God create you, Holy Mary!
And re-created you, through a sacred painting,
In this, our Bishopric.

Delicately was your image painted
And on the sacred canvas, your soul was concealed.
All is perfect and complete in its presence,
And there, God willing, I shall dwell for ever.

Who will follow my example?
Who will hasten to come after me?
Oh, let us kneel round about her!
Let us sing sweet songs
And scatter flowers in her presence!

Weeping, I commune with my own soul,
That the whole purpose of my soul may be made known,
And that the desire of my heart may be fulfilled
In the building of the Virgin's house.
Then shall my soul be at rest there.

And it shall know perfume greater than the fragrance of flowers
And my hymn will rise in praise of the beautiful bloom
Which forms her perpetual adornment!

The flower of the cocoa spreads in fragrance.
The flower of the pomoya perfume every road
Leading to this holy place.
And there I, the sweet singer, will dwell.
Hark, O harken to my hymn of joy!

TILMA

Marty Rotella and Ed Sansanelli

One day an Indian, an Aztec Indian,
Walking on a road beheld a lovely lady, and she said
Climb to the top of this hill,
There you will see Castilian flowers.

Pick them, gather them, bundle them,
Then bring them down to me, in your Tilma.
A mantle, a cape, a garment, a robe,
A woven cloak, a Tilma.

Imagine gathering flowers in December,
They're not in sight nor in season,
These flowers are the proof you need,
The sign you're to carry to the Bishop.

A picture of love, an image of faith,
A portrait of hope, a Tilma.
Bishop Zumarraga said, "unfurl",
Your cloak given to the world.

The roses fell, the Tilma showed,
Our Lady for all to know.
A picture of love, an image of faith,
A portrait of hope, a Tilma.

From musical audio cassette tape *I Wait on Tepeyac* available
from Publisher.

OUR LADY OF GUADALUPE

You are the fountain of my life
Under your shadow and in your protection,
I fear no evil, no pain, no worry.

Refrain

Here, in the crossing of your arms
Could there be anything else that I need?
Nothing discourage, nothing depress me.

Refrain

You are the star of the ocean
My boat is small and the waves are so high,
But with you to guide me, I'll reach my homeland.

Refrain

You are the dawn of a new day
For you give birth to the Son of the Father.
All of my lifetime, I'll walk beside you.

Refrain:

O Maria, O most merciful Mother
Gentle Virgin with the name Guadalupe,
On a mountain we find roses in winter,
All the world has been touched by your love.

APPENDIX O

AN INSPIRED PLEA
FROM OUR LADY OF GUADALUPE
Daniel J. Lynch

I am the Perfect and Perpetual Ever-Virgin Mary. I was conceived without original sin and committed no actual sin. My virginity was preserved before, during and after the birth of my only Child, my Son, Jesus Christ, true God and true Man. My virginity was preserved during His birth because He miraculously emerged from my womb just as He miraculously resurrected from His tomb. I had no other children and never had sexual relations either before or after His birth. See Mt 1:23, 25.

I am the Mother of the One True God, Jesus Christ, Lord of all and one of three Divine Persons with the Father and the Holy Spirit who share the Divine Nature and in whom we live and move and have our being. See Acts 17:28.

God is your Creator. He is goodness and love (see 1 Jn 16) and He so loved the world as to give it through me His only begotten Son so that you might be saved from the everlasting fires of hell and the Kingdom of Satan for eternal life and happiness in the Kingdom of God by the forgiveness of your repented sins. See Jn 3:16; 1 Jn 9.

Come to Him all of you who find life burdensome and He will give you rest. His burden is light and He is meek and humble of heart. See Mt 11:28. He stands knocking at the door of your heart. Won't you open it and let Him in? See Rev 3:20.

In me, God finds his original creative design intact. I am the New Eve and perfectly conform to God's original plan of a sinless humanity. See Gn 3:15. I can help you!

From the moment of my conception, as a result of natural sexual intercourse between my parents, I am full of grace. See Lk 1:28, 1:41. This is my Immaculate Conception. By a divine privilege I was preserved by God from all stain of sin both original and actual during my entire life on earth. As a consequence of my Immaculate Conception, my body did not undergo corruption but I was assumed body and soul into heaven. See Ps 16:10-11. I am now in heaven in my glorified body in the heart of the Blessed Trinity.

Because of my Divine Motherhood and cooperation in God's plan for your salvation as Co-Redemptrix and Mediatrix of All Graces, I am by grace Queen of heaven and earth, of angels and men. See Lk 1:32.

Because of your sins of abortion and the rejection of God's graces of conversion, my heart is pierced with a sword of sorrow. See Lk 2:35.

I am the Universal Mother of all humanity. See Ps 87:5. I carry the pain of your sins in my Sorrowful and Immaculate Heart. I intercede with my Son for your conversion. Do not alienate the souls of the little ones from me. See Mt 19:14. It would be better that a millstone be hung around your head than to alienate them from me. Do not abuse my images which represent my presence among you. If you venerate and honor them, you venerate and honor me. As I am but a creature of God, when you venerate me you glorify God as I did by my Magnificat Canticle of Praise to Him. See Lk 1:46.

Venerate my images and I will manifest to you my love as your merciful Mother, I will give you my help and my protection from the wickedness and snares of the Devil.

Come to Jesus through me. Abandon yourselves totally! Consecrate yourselves to my Sorrowful and Immaculate Heart. I will help you! Have confidence in me. Fear nothing. Am I not your Mother? Are you not under my shadow and protection? Is there anything else that you need?

I will hear your cries and relieve your sufferings. I too suffered as your Co-Redemptrix for your salvation. I united all of my sufferings with those of my Son Jesus on His Cross. I am your fountain of life, the Mediatrix between you and Jesus of all of your prayers and sacrifices to Him and of all of Jesus' graces to you. I am His greatest gift to you. See Jn 19:27.

But will Jesus find any faith when he returns to the world? See Lk 18:8. I want abortion to end now! I want you to convert to God now! But I need your help!

Please give me your prayers and sacrifices in reparation for the sins of the world and I will magnify them for God so that His grace and mercy will descend on the earth. Then the Kingdom of God will come as a universal reign of grace, beauty, harmony, holiness and peace! Do everything as best as you can!

APPENDIX P

DECLARATION OF HUMAN LIFE

We hold that these truths are divinely revealed or are evident from the exercise of right reason:

1. God our Creator is the Author of human life.

2. Human life is unique and endowed with dignity, freedom and individual rights.

3. Human life consists of the integrated union in a person of a mortal physical body and an immortal spiritual soul.

4. Human life begins by God's creative act with the cooperation of man and woman from the instant of union of spermatazoa and ovum within the body of a woman. It ends with the cessation of heart and respiratory function.

5. God's purpose in creating human life is to share His infinite goodness in His own image. Men and women thus have the duty to glorify God through praise, thanksgiving, in service and love. We should cooperate with His grace and try to know Him, obey His will and fulfill His plan for our lives. This will culminate in eternal union with Him.

6. Men and women were orginally created by God in the persons of Adam and Eve in a supernatural state of immortality. They had the gift of integrity or absence of conflict betwen the dictates of right reason and passions. These gifts were lost through their personal sin of disobedience to God's command. Because of this, death and sin have since been naturally transmitted to every man and woman at the moment of their creation.

7. All men and women have been redeemed from death and sin through the personal sacrificial passion and death of Jesus Christ, one Divine person with both human and Divine natures. He has merited for us eternal life through the forgiveness of repented sins.

8. God's will is that only men and women united in marriage cooperate with Him in the procreation of human life from the beginning to the end of conjugal union.

9. God has given men and women a total and compatible integrated sexuality including the power of cooperative genital activity which gives them the power to unite and procreate in cooperation with Him.

10. It is morally wrong for men or women to interfere with God's will for the procreation of the human race under any circumstances either by artificial insemination, contraception, abortion, infanticide, sterilization, euthanasia, homosexuality, masturbation, fornication, adultery, divorce and remarriage, suicide, genocide, and eugenic engineering.

11. The life of the celibate person is equal in dignity to that of the married person.

12. After the personal death of a man or woman, God particularly judges the soul. Those who die in the state of grace with perfect charity will promptly and eternally join Him in heaven. Those without such perfect penance, but of good will after purification in Purgatory, will also eternally join God in heaven. Those who die in the state of mortal sin without repentance will promptly go to eternal hell.

13. At the end of the world, the mortal bodies of deceased men and women will be resurrected and eternally rejoined with their immortal souls and Jesus Christ will make a general eternal judgment of each person according to his works before all souls who will see with them, living and dead, their good works, their sins and their societal effects.

14. Parents have the primary duty to educate their children in these truths and their moral and biological aspects and the primary duty to supervise, control and care for their children.

15. The state has no right to legislate, declare, enforce, support, encourage or educate anything contrary to these truths and the moral and biological aspects thereof.

APPENDIX Q

POPE JOHN PAUL II'S PRAYER FROM *THE GOSPEL OF LIFE*

O Mary,
bright dawn of the new world,
Mother of the living,
to you do we entrust the *cause of life:*
Look down, O Mother,
upon the vast numbers
of babies not allowed to be born,
of the poor whose lives are made difficult,
of men and women
who are victims of brutal violence,
of the elderly and the sick killed
by indifference or out of misguided mercy.
Grant that all who believe in your Son
may *proclaim the Gospel of life*
with honesty and love
to the people of our time.
Obtain for them the grace
to *accept* that Gospel
as a gift ever new,
the joy *of celebrating* it with gratitude
throughout their lives
and the courage to *bear witness to it*
resolutely, in order to build,
together with all people of good will,
the civilization of truth and love,
to the praise and glory of God,
the Creator and lover of life. Amen.

APPENDIX R

BIBLIOGRAPHY

In Chronological Order:

Our Lady of Guadalupe, Patroness of the Americas: Fr. George Lee. (Catholic Book Publishing Co., New York, 1897 and 1947).

The Dark Virgin: Donald Demarest and Coley Taylor (Coley Taylor, Inc., Porter's Landing, Freeport, Maine, 1956).

Our Lady of Guadalupe the Hope of America: (Our Lady of Guadalupe Trappist Abbey, Lafayette, Oregon, 1961).

America's Treasure: Helen Behrens (Apartado 26 732, Mexico 14 D.F., 1964).

A Handbook on Guadalupe: C.J. Wahlig and co-authors (Franciscan Marytown Press, Kenosha, Wisconsin, 1974).

The Wonder of Guadalupe: Francis Johnston (Tan Books and Publishers, Inc., Rockford, Illinois 61105, 1981).

Our Lady of Guadalupe and The Conquest of Darkness: Warren H. Carroll (Christendom Publications, Rt. 3, Box 87, Front Royal, Virginia 22630, 1983).

Mother of the Americas: Robert Feeney (Aquinas Press, Forest Grove, Oregon, 1989).

Mary of the Americas: Christopher Rengers (Alba House, Staten Island, New York, 1989).